B LOOM'S

ReViews

COMPREHENSIVE \ RESEARCH & STUDY GUIDES

William Shakespeare's
Macbeth

Edited & with
an Introduction
by Harold Bloom

First Printing
1 3 5 7 9 8 6 4 2

ISBN: 0-7910-3677-4 (hc)
     0-7910-4136-0 (pb)

Chelsea House Publishers
1974 Sproul Road, Suite 400
P.O. Box 914
Broomall, PA 19008-0914

Contents

Editor's Note   4

Introduction   5

Biography of William Shakespeare   8

Thematic and Structural Analysis   13

List of Characters   24

Critical Views
   Samuel Johnson: The Flaws and Virtues of the Play   27
   William Hazlitt: Macbeth and Richard III   27
   Samuel Taylor Coleridge: *Macbeth* and *Hamlet*   31
   Victor Hugo: Macbeth as Hunger   33
   A. C. Bradley: The Use of Prose in *Macbeth*   35
   Sigmund Freud: Macbeth as Parricide   37
   G. Wilson Knight: Fear, Evil, and Nightmare in the Play   39
   M. C. Bradbrook: The Sources for the Play   43
   L. C. Knights: The Violation of Nature in the Play   45
   John Berryman: Lady Macbeth   47
   Marilyn French: Gender Roles in the Play   50
   Lisa Low: Why We Are Drawn to Macbeth   53
   John Turner: Macbeth's Hubris   56
   Barbara Everett: The Macbeths as a Married Couple   59
   Charles and Michelle Martindale: Death in the Play   61
   Nicholas Grene: The Witches   64
   Garry Wills: *Macbeth* and the Gunpowder Plot   66

Works by William Shakespeare   69

Works about William Shakespeare and *Macbeth*   72

Index of Themes and Ideas   77

Editor's Note

My Introduction centers upon Macbeth's uncannily powerful imagination, which leads him only further into terrible crimes, yet also draws our sympathy, despite our moral revulsion. Dr. Samuel Johnson, in the first of the critical views, asserts otherwise, since he sees only courage (and not fantasy-making power) as Macbeth's virtue. William Hazlitt, the great Romantic critic, accurately sees that we never lose our concern for Macbeth. Coleridge, juxtaposing Hamlet and Macbeth, finds Macbeth's essence in the witches: "the imaginative disconnected from the good."

The French romantic poet Victor Hugo strikingly associates Macbeth with the biblical Nimrod, first hunter of men. In A. C. Bradley's fine perception, prose in the text of *Macbeth* always represents insanity or some borderline disorder. Sigmund Freud, shrewder on *Macbeth* than on *Hamlet*, finds the Oedipal pattern of parricide in the play.

George Wilson Knight, a great if uneven interpreter of Shakespeare, regards Macbeth as a monster of isolation, while Muriel Bradbrook shows how gorgeously Shakespeare elaborated the sources of this play.

A Formalist critic, L. C. Knights, judges Macbeth to be primarily an offender against nature, which is much the verdict upon Lady Macbeth by the American poet John Berryman.

In Feminist critiques, Marilyn French rather surprisingly holds that Shakespeare portrays Lady Macbeth as being more demonic than her husband, while Lisa Low returns us to our deep if disconcerting sympathy for Macbeth. Barbara Everett, in a powerful reading, traces the disaster of the Macbeths to their authentic love for one another.

The Martindales, rather surprisingly to me, find much of the Stoic attitude towards death in *Macbeth*, after which Nicholas Grene illuminates the function of the Witches in the play. In a final extract, the political historian Garry Wills perhaps overstates the effect upon *Macbeth* of the notorious Gunpowder Plot of 1605, in which Catholic rebels attempted to destroy King James and his government.

Introduction

HAROLD BLOOM

Macbeth ought to be the least sympathetic of Shakespeare's hero-villains. He is a murderer of old men, women, and children, and has a particular obsession with overcoming time by murdering the future: hence his failed attempt to kill Fleance, and his successful slaughter of Macduff's children. And yet the playgoer and the reader cannot resist identifying with the imagination of Macbeth. A great killing-machine, Macbeth has few attributes beyond imagination to recommend him, and that imagination itself is anything but benign. Yet it is open to the powers of the air and of the night: occult, mediumlike, prophetic, and moral at least in part, it must be the most singular imagination in all of Shakespeare's plays. And yet it has great limitations; it is not much allied to Macbeth's far more ordinary, indeed inadequate intellectual powers. Its autonomy, together with its desperate strength, is what destroys all of Macbeth's victims, and at last Macbeth himself. Imagination or "fantasy" is an equivocal term in the Renaissance, where it can mean both poetic furor, a personal replacement for divine inspiration, and a loss-in-reality, perhaps as a consequence of such a displacement of sacred by secular.

Shakespeare has no single position in regard to the fantasy-making power, whether in *Macbeth* or in *A Midsummer Night's Dream* or *The Tempest*. Yet all these are visionary dramas, and in some sense pragmatically exalt imagination even as they question it. But *Macbeth* is a tragedy, and a visionary tragedy is a strange genre. Like Hamlet, Othello, and Lear, Macbeth is a tragic protagonist, and yet like Claudius, Iago, and Edmund, Macbeth is a villain, indeed a monster of murderousness far surpassing the others. We find it difficult, as we read or watch a performance of *Macbeth,* to think of its protagonist as a criminal dictator, a small-scale Hitler or Stalin, and yet he is pragmatically just that. I do not think that Macbeth's wistful scruples, his nostalgias and regrets, draw us to him; he is never in any danger of collapsing back into the innocence he rarely ceases to crave. The reader and playgoer needs to ask: "Why, even in despite of myself, do I identify with Macbeth, down to the very end?" It cannot be that Macbeth's desires and ambitions essentially are our own; even if the Oedipal desire to slay the father (the good King Duncan) is universal. Even if we are all would-be usurpers, most of us presumably do not desire to terrorize our societies. The appeal of Macbeth, hardly to be resisted, seems to me at the heart of Shakespeare's concerns in this great domestic tragedy of blood.

Macbeth's imagination is at once his greatest strength and his destructive weakness, yet it does not provoke an ambivalence in us. We thrill to its poetic, expressionistic strength, whatever its consequences. Shakespeare, on some level, may be making a critique of his own imagination, which has much in common with Macbeth's, and yet the play is anything but a condemnation of the Macbethian imagination. Indeed, as Macbeth increasingly becomes outraged by the equivocal nature of the occult promises that have been made to him, his sense of being outraged contaminates us, so that we come to share in his outrage. He becomes our paradigm of confounded expectations, and we are moved by him as we are moved by Captain Ahab, who in Melville's *Moby-Dick* plays the role of an American Macbeth. Ahab is not a murderer, and yet his obsessive hunt for *Moby-Dick* destroys the *Pequod* and its entire crew, except for the storytelling Ishmael. Melville modeled Ahab's imagination upon Macbeth's, and a close comparison of Ahab and Macbeth is capable of illuminating both figures. Like Ahab, Macbeth is made into a monomaniac by his compulsive imagination, though killing King Duncan has little in common with the vain attempt to kill the White Whale, who has maimed poor Ahab. Still, like Ahab, Macbeth attempts to strike through the mask of natural appearances in order to uncover the malign principles that, at least in part, would seem to govern the universe. The cosmos, both in Shakespeare's play and in Melville's prose-epic, seems to have resulted from a creation that was also a fall. Both Macbeth and Ahab are central and appropriate to their universes; their imaginings of disaster bring about fresh disasters, and their battles against their own sense of having been outraged by supernatural forces bring about cataclysmic disorders, both for themselves and nearly everyone else about them.

The comparison between Macbeth and his descendant Ahab has its limits. Ahab's guilt is only that of an instrument; he leads his crew to destruction, but he himself is neither a tyrant nor a usurper. Macbeth, a far greater figure than Shakespeare's Richard III or his Claudius, nevertheless is in their tradition: he is a plotter and an assassin. And yet he has sublimity; an authentic tragic grandeur touches and transfigures him. That difference arises again from the nature and power of his prophetic imagination, which is far too strong for every other faculty in him to battle. Macbeth's mind, character, affections are all helpless when confronted by the strength and prevalence of his fantasy, which does his thinking, judging, and feeling for him. Before he scarcely is conscious of a desire, wish, or ambition, the image of the accomplished deed already dominates him, long before the act is performed. Macbeth *sees,* sometimes quite literally, the phantasmagoria of the future. He is an involuntary visionary, and there is something baffling about his ambition to become king. What do he and Lady Macbeth wish to do with their royal status and power, once they have it? An evening with King and Queen Macbeth at court is an affair apocalyptically dismal: the frightened Thanes brood as to just who will be murdered next, and the graciousness of their hostess seems adequately represented by her famous dismissal to stay not upon the order of their going, but go! Whether the Macbeths still hope for progeny is ambiguous, as is the question of whether they have had children who then died, but they seem to share a dread of futurity. Macbeth's horror of time, often remarked by his critics, has a crucial relation to his uncanniest aspect, transcending fantasy, because he seems to sense a realm free of time yet at least as much a nightmare as his time-obsessed existence. Something in Macbeth really is most at home in the world of the witches and of Hecate. Against the positive transcendence of Hamlet's charismatic personality, Shakespeare set the negative transcendence of Macbeth's hag-ridden nature. And yet a negative transcendence remains a transcendence; there are no flights of angels to herald the end of Macbeth, but there is the occult breakthrough that persuades us, at last, that the time is free. ❖

Biography of William Shakespeare

Few events in the life of William Shakespeare are supported by reliable evidence, and many incidents recorded by commentators of the last four centuries are either conjectural or apocryphal.

William Shakespeare was born in Stratford-upon-Avon on April 22 or 23, 1564, the son of Mary Arden and John Shakespeare, a tradesman. His very early education was in the hands of a tutor, for his parents were probably illiterate. At age seven he entered the Free School in Stratford, where he learned the "small Latin and less Greek" attributed to him by Ben Jonson. When not in school Shakespeare may have gone to the popular Stratford fairs and to the dramas and mystery plays performed by traveling actors.

When Shakespeare was about thirteen his father removed him from school and apprenticed him to a butcher, although it is not known how long he remained in this occupation. When he was eighteen he married Anne Hathaway; their first child, Susanna, was born six months later. A pair of twins, Hamnet and Judith, were born in February 1585. About this time Shakespeare was caught poaching deer on the estate of Sir Thomas Lucy of Cherlecot; Lucy's prosecution is said to have inspired Shakespeare to write his earliest literary work, a satire on his opponent. Shakespeare was convicted of poaching and forced to leave Stratford. He withdrew to London, leaving his family behind. He soon attached himself to the stage, initially in a menial capacity (as tender of playgoers' horses, according to one tradition), then as prompter's attendant. When the poaching furor subsided, Shakespeare returned to Stratford to join one of the many bands of itinerant actors. In the next five years he gained what little theatre training he received.

By 1592 Shakespeare was a recognized actor, and in that year he wrote and produced his first play, *Henry the Sixth, Part One.* Its success impelled Shakespeare soon afterward to write the second and third parts of *Henry the Sixth.* (Many early and modern critics believe that *Love's Labour's Lost* preceded these histories as Shakespeare's earliest play, but the majority of modern scholars discount this theory.) Shakespeare's popularity provoked the jealousy of Robert Greene, as recorded in his posthumous *Groats-worth of Wit* (1592).

In 1593 Shakespeare published *Venus and Adonis,* a long poem based upon Ovid (or perhaps upon Arthur Golding's translation of Ovid's *Metamorphoses*). It was dedicated to the young Earl of Southampton—but perhaps without permission, a possible indication that Shakespeare was trying to gain the nobleman's patronage. However, the dedicatory address to Southampton in the poem *The Rape of Lucrece* (1594) reveals Shakespeare to have been on good terms with him. Many plays—such as *Titus Andronicus, The Comedy of Errors,* and *Romeo and Juliet*—were produced over the next several years, most performed by Shakespeare's troupe, the Lord Chamberlain's Company. In December 1594 Shakespeare acted in a comedy (of unknown authorship) before Queen Elizabeth; many other royal performances followed in the next decade.

In August 1596 Shakespeare's son Hamnet died. Early the next year Shakespeare bought a home, New Place, in the center of Stratford; he is said to have planted a mulberry tree in the back yard with his own hands. Shakespeare's relative prosperity is indicated by his purchasing more than a hundred acres of farmland in 1602, a cottage near his estate later that year, and half-interest in the tithes of some local villages in 1605.

In September 1598 Shakespeare began his friendship with the then unknown Ben Jonson by producing his play *Every Man in His Humour.* The next year the publisher William Jaggard affixed Shakespeare's name, without his permission, to a curious medley of poems under the title *The Passionate Pilgrim;* the majority of the poems were not by Shakespeare. Two of his sonnets, however, appeared in this collection, although the 154 sonnets, with their mysterious dedication to "Mr. W. H.," were not published as a group until 1609. Also in 1599 the Globe Theatre was built in Southwark (an area of London), and Shakespeare's company began acting there. Many of his greatest plays—*Troilus and Cressida, King Lear, Othello, Macbeth*—

were performed in the Globe before its destruction by fire in 1613.

The death in 1603 of Queen Elizabeth, the last of the Tudors, and the accession of James I, from the Stuart dynasty of Scotland, created anxiety throughout England. Shakespeare's fortunes, however, were unaffected, as the new monarch extended the license of Shakespeare's company to perform at the Globe. James I saw a performance of *Othello* at the court in November 1604. In October 1605 Shakespeare's company performed before the Mayor and Corporation of Oxford.

The last five years of Shakespeare's life seem void of incident; he had retired from the stage by 1613. Among the few known incidents is Shakespeare's involvement in a heated and lengthy dispute about the enclosure of common-fields around Stratford. He died on April 23, 1616, and was buried in the Church of St. Mary's in Stratford. A monument was later erected to him in the Poets' Corner of Westminster Abbey.

Numerous corrupt quarto editions of Shakespeare's plays were published during his lifetime. These editions, based either on manuscripts, prompt-books, or sometimes merely actors' recollections of the plays, were meant to capitalize on Shakespeare's renown. Other plays, now deemed wholly or largely spurious—*Edward the Third, The Yorkshire Tragedy, The Two Noble Kinsmen,* and others—were also published under Shakespeare's name during and after his lifetime. Shakespeare's plays were collected in the First Folio of 1623 by John Heminge and Henry Condell. Nine years later the Second Folio was published, and in 1640 Shakespeare's poems were collected. The first standard collected edition was by Nicholas Rowe (1709), followed by the editions of Alexander Pope (1725), Lewis Theobald (1733), Samuel Johnson (1765), Edmond Malone (1790), and many others.

Shakespeare's plays are now customarily divided into the following categories (probable dates of writing are given in brackets): comedies (*The Comedy of Errors* [1590], *The Taming of the Shrew* [1592], *The Two Gentlemen of Verona* [1592–93], *A Midsummer Night's Dream* [1595], *Love's Labour's Lost* [1595], *The Merchant of Venice* [1596–98], *As You Like It*

[1597], *The Merry Wives of Windsor* [1597], *Much Ado About Nothing* [1598–99], *Twelfth Night* [1601], *All's Well That Ends Well* [1603–04], and *Measure for Measure* [1604]); histories (*Henry the Sixth, Part One* [1590–92], *Henry the Sixth, Parts Two and Three* [1590–92], *Richard the Third* [1591], *King John* [1591–98], *Richard the Second* [1595], *Henry the Fourth, Part One* [1597], *Henry the Fourth, Part Two* [1597], *Henry the Fifth* [1599], and *Henry the Eighth* [1613]); tragedies (*Titus Andronicus* [1590], *Romeo and Juliet* [1595], *Julius Caesar* [1599], *Hamlet* [1599–1601], *Troilus and Cressida* [1602], *Othello* [1602–04], *King Lear* [1604–05], *Macbeth* [1606], *Timon of Athens* [1607], *Antony and Cleopatra* [1606–07], and *Coriolanus* [1608]); romances (*Pericles, Prince of Tyre* [1606–08], *Cymbeline* [1609–10], *The Winter's Tale* [1610–11], and *The Tempest* [1611]). However, Shakespeare willfully defied the canons of classical drama by mingling comedy, tragedy, and history, so that in some cases classification is debatable or arbitrary.

Shakespeare's reputation, while subject to many fluctuations, was firmly established by the eighteenth century. Samuel Johnson remarked: "Perhaps it would not be easy to find any authour, except Homer, who invented so much as Shakespeare, who so much advanced the studies which he cultivated, who effused so much novelty upon his age or country. The form, the characters, the language, and the shows of the English drama are his." Early in the nineteenth century Samuel Taylor Coleridge declared: "The Englishman who without reverence, a proud and affectionate reverence, can utter the name of William Shakespeare, stands disqualified for the office of critic. . . . Great as was the genius of Shakespeare, his judgment was at least equal to it."

A curious controversy developed in the middle of the nineteenth century in regard to the authorship of Shakespeare's plays, some contending that Sir Francis Bacon was the actual author of the plays, others (including Mark Twain) advancing the claims of the Earl of Oxford. None of these attempts has succeeded in persuading the majority of scholars that Shakespeare himself is not the author of the plays attributed to him.

In recent years many landmark editions of Shakespeare, with increasingly accurate texts and astute critical commentary, have emerged. These include the New Cambridge Shakespeare (1931–66) and the New Arden Shakespeare (1951f.). Such critics as T. S. Eliot, G. Wilson Knight, Northrop Frye, W. H. Auden, and many others have continued to elucidate Shakespeare, his work, and his times, and he remains the most written-about author in the history of English literature. ❖

Thematic and Structural Analysis

William Shakespeare's *Macbeth* begins tumultuously, with the meeting of three witches in a thunderstorm. The witches, or Weird Sisters, make plans to reconvene shortly in order to meet Macbeth. This startling scene, consisting only of a brief, incantatory exchange, is seemingly extraneous to the play's action. It functions, however, as an important introduction to the play's main plot. For, in addition to setting an ominous mood, this scene immerses its audience in a world presided over by enigmatic and terrifying forces, a world in which nature itself is violent and tempestuous. The association between the witches and the storm makes thematic sense as well, for both represent a kind of threatening power beyond human control; whenever the witches reappear later in the play, the stage directions call for thunder.

The play's **second scene** shifts the focus to a more worldly form of violence and disorder: political warfare. The scene is set in a military camp, where King Duncan of Scotland—together with his sons Malcolm and Donalbain and a retinue of nobles and attendants—awaits the outcome of a battle against an army of rebels. A captain from the royal army, wounded and covered in blood, arrives with news from the front. He tells of the heroic exploits of "brave Macbeth," who, fighting at the head of the king's army, personally slew the rebel Macdonwald. The captain also informs Duncan that the rebel forces have been reinforced by a Norwegian army. Faint from loss of blood, the captain cannot satisfy the king's curiosity about this redoubled attack on his army, but fortunately the Thane of Rosse ("Thane" is an honorific title like "Earl" or "Lord") arrives with further news. The King of Norway has indeed attacked, and has in fact been assisted by still another rebel, the Thane of Cawdor. Nevertheless, Rosse announces, the uprising has been defeated and the principal traitors captured. Duncan orders the execution of the treasonous Thane of Cawdor, and—to reward the valor of his general—bestows the vacated title Thane of Cawdor upon Macbeth.

The juxtaposition between these opening scenes is a striking example of Shakespeare's dramatic technique. Though the two scenes are set in completely different milieux, there is between them a powerful continuity of mood. The violence of the reported battle, the tangible evidence of bloodshed provided by the wounded captain, and the general air of anxiety hanging over the camp, make this second scene as unsettling as the first. Taken together, the two scenes give the distinct impression that the world of the play is in a general state of upheaval, as if the storm, the witches, and the political rebellion are all somehow associated with one another. This ominous impression tempers somewhat the optimistic conclusion of the second scene, in which, after all, the rebellion has been defeated. Can one trust this restored social order while the witches are still at large? The answer turns out to be no, for in the play's third scene the witches overtly interfere with the political world, setting the play's main tragic plot in motion.

In the **third scene,** the witches are joined on stage by two of the triumphant generals of Duncan's army, Banquo and Macbeth. The three witches greet Macbeth three times: as Thane of Glamis—his accustomed title; as Thane of Cawdor—a title the audience knows has been given to Macbeth, but which Macbeth himself has no reason to expect; finally, they address Macbeth as one "that shalt be King hereafter." The witches also promise that though Banquo will never be a king, his sons will rule. With this, the three witches vanish, leaving Macbeth and Banquo to grapple with the grand destinies foreseen for them. As they are doing so, emissaries from Duncan arrive bearing word of the king's gratitude, and Macbeth learns that he has been made Thane of Cawdor. This seems to confirm the witches' predictions, and consequently to imply that Macbeth himself will supplant Duncan as king. The immediate question, of course, is how? Prompted by a budding ambition, Macbeth begins to imagine regicide.

The psychic costs of this murderous ambition are considerable, and in fact the corrosive effect of ambition is one of the major themes of the play. Having imagined the murder of Duncan, Macbeth is immediately stricken by what we today would call a crisis of conscience: his ambitious desire comes into conflict with a powerfully felt sense of duty. The speeches in which he articulates his ambivalence—here and in the scenes to come—are choppy and often confusing, manifesting the real difficulty of Macbeth's inner conflict. In order to understand the magnitude of the crime Macbeth contemplates, it is important to remember that in the early seventeenth century, when *Macbeth* was written and first performed, kingship was thought of as a sacred institution, and the king was seen as God's representative on earth. Consequently, killing a king would not only break the law but would also be seen as a violation of a natural social order. Moreover, Macbeth's regicidal fantasy, by shaking his fundamental obedience to the state, calls into question all of the assumptions upon which he had hitherto based his actions. Macbeth himself puts it like this:

> My thought, whose murther yet is but fantastical,
> Shakes so my single state of man,
> That function is smother'd in surmise. . . .

Simply put, it is hard for Macbeth to know how to act once his basic values—loyalty, duty, honor, rank—have been upset by his growing ambition.

Act 1, Scene 4, further explores Macbeth's inner crisis by juxtaposing his "black and deep desires" with the ceremonial, public language in which Duncan praises his victorious officers. Duncan is established as a good and gracious king—loving, generous, and eager to reward his subjects—which makes Macbeth's contemplated regicide seem all the more horrifying. At the same time, Duncan names his son Malcolm as his successor, which fuels Macbeth's treasonous imagination, making it clear that the succession will not fall on him in the normal course of events. Duncan and his entire retinue head toward Macbeth's castle at Inverness for a celebratory visit.

Act 1, Scene 5, introduces Lady Macbeth, who from this point on is Macbeth's partner in crime. After reading a letter from Macbeth describing the witches' prophesy, Lady Macbeth expresses concern that her husband will be unable to kill Duncan: he is too full of the "milk of human kindness," and so she vows to goad him on to murder. Macbeth arrives, and she proposes that Duncan be killed that night. When Duncan and

Banquo arrive at Inverness (**Act 1, Scene 6**), Lady Macbeth demonstrates her capacity for deceit, giving them a very polite welcome despite her murderous intent.

With the prospect of regicide suddenly made more immediate, Macbeth's internal crisis intensifies still further (**1.7**). Now, however, Lady Macbeth is there to denounce his hesitations as cowardice and to bolster his failing resolve. In a series of uniquely violent and horrifying speeches, she challenges Macbeth's manhood and outlines her plan to kill Duncan and seize the throne. In particular, she proposes that the two grooms guarding the king's chamber be drugged with wine and subsequently framed for the murder. Macbeth acquiesces to the plan as the first act comes to a close.

The **second act** begins in darkness; night has fallen and the murder of Duncan is therefore imminent. Banquo and his son Fleance enter with torches, and we learn that Banquo, like Macbeth, has been rendered sleepless by "cursed thoughts" occasioned by the witches' promises. Macbeth enters, and the two generals speak briefly of the prophesy. Macbeth hints that he will have a favor to ask of Banquo, and the latter answers that he will be glad to help so long as he is able to keep his honor intact and his "allegiance clear." The point here is that unlike Macbeth, Banquo maintains his sense of duty. As soon as Banquo and Fleance leave the stage, Macbeth has a vision of a dagger in the air, pointing him toward Duncan's chamber. Macbeth cannot tell if this is an oracular sign or merely "a false creation, / Proceeding from the heat-oppressed brain," and his hallucinatory uncertainty here marks the extreme point of his mental crisis. With a horrified and numb resolve, Macbeth goes to murder the king.

As Macbeth kills Duncan offstage, Lady Macbeth awaits him (**2.2**). Macbeth enters, carrying the bloody daggers, obviously shaken by the enormity of his crime. Lady Macbeth is forced to take the daggers from him in order to ensure that the chamber grooms are properly framed. A knocking at the castle gate brings events to a crisis, but as Lady Macbeth hurries to wash the blood from their hands and restore the appearance of normalcy, Macbeth remains in his state of shock, saying "To know my deed, 'twere best not know myself."

The suspense of this critical moment is extended by a brilliantly macabre comic interlude at the beginning of **Act 2, Scene 3,** in which the knocking at the gate is answered by a porter, who delivers a prolonged and amusing monologue. At last he opens the door to admit Macduff and Lennox—two more of the king's generals—who banter briefly with him before Macbeth's entrance. As Macduff goes to call on the king, Lennox and Macbeth engage in some extremely portentous small talk: Lennox complains that a terrible storm had taken place during the night. The audience associates this storm—whose winds Lennox says sounded like "strange screams of death"—with the murder of Duncan (itself a disruption of natural order), as well as with the storms previously linked to the witches themselves. Macduff reenters with news of the murder ("O horror! horror! horror!") and the castle is thrown into a state of confusion. It is reported that Macbeth, in a feigned rage, has slaughtered the two grooms of Duncan's chamber, thereby preventing investigation. In a hurried conversation, the king's two sons (Malcolm and Donalbain) agree that they themselves are put in danger by this assassination, and agree to flee from Scotland.

The **final scene in Act 2** takes place outside of Macbeth's castle, as Rosse and an unnamed old man discuss the unnatural events of the previous evening. It seems that Duncan's horses have broken out of their stalls in the night, and—as the old man reports—"'Tis said, they eat each other." This report confirms the sense conveyed by Lennox's description of the evening's storm in Act 2, Scene 3: namely, that the murder of Duncan is a serious violation of natural order with widely felt repercussions. Macduff, bringing news for Rosse, sums up for the audience the immediate results of the previous evening's violence. He reports that since Malcolm and Donalbain have fled, they are thought to have been accomplices to the murder. The crown, as promised by the witches, falls to Macbeth.

Act 3 begins with Banquo musing on these events. Knowing the prophesy as he does, Banquo suspects that Macbeth may have had a hand in Duncan's murder. Macbeth and Lady Macbeth enter in order to request Banquo's presence at a feast in the evening, and Banquo promises that he will attend after spending the day riding with Fleance. Bothered by the idea that Banquo's descendants will be kings, and threatened by Banquo's knowledge of the witches' prophesy, Macbeth promptly hires two assassins to kill Banquo and his son.

Macbeth has a good political reason to fear Banquo, who in fact already suspects Macbeth of engineering Duncan's murder. What is odd here is that Macbeth should suddenly be concerned with the promised royalty of Banquo's line. In a long soliloquy, Macbeth describes himself as fruitless and barren, and complains bitterly that he should have killed Duncan only in order to put Banquo's sons on the throne. This is somewhat paradoxical. For one thing, Macbeth knew all along that the witches promised the crown to Banquo's line. Why does this become a problem only after Macbeth takes the throne? For another, there is no reason to believe that Macbeth himself has any children to pass the crown on to, nor that his ambition had hitherto been directed toward the founding of a royal line. Why should Macbeth care that Banquo's heirs will be kings? They are not going to displace any children of Macbeth's. One provisional answer to this unresolved question is that ambition in this play is a fundamentally unstable mental state: having the kingship, Macbeth inevitably wants more. Alternatively, one could say that the future ascendancy of Banquo's sons—since it is clearly beyond Macbeth's control—marks a limit to Macbeth's power, and that consequently it chafes him. In **Act 3, Scene 2,** we find that for Lady Macbeth, too, the realization of her ambitions has failed to bring contentment.

Banquo is killed by the murderers in **Act 3, Scene 3,** but Fleance manages to get away. When, during the evening's banquet, one of the killers tells Macbeth of Fleance's escape, it corroborates once more the witches' promise to Banquo (**3.4**). Macbeth exclaims

> Then comes my fit again: I had else been perfect;
> Whole as the marble, founded as the rock,
> As broad and general as the casing air:
> But now, I am cabin'd, cribb'd, confin'd, bound in
> To saucy doubts and fears.

This blurted speech confirms that in some sense the promise made to Banquo's offspring signifies for Macbeth a limit to his own power. He wants to be perfect —as eternal as marble and as all-encompassing as air—but the unavoidable prospect of being replaced by Banquo's descendants reminds Macbeth of the limits of his power and control. Or, more broadly, one might say that the threat of Banquo's line, by underscoring the anticipated end of his own lineage, reminds Macbeth of his mortality.

The feast in **Act 3, Scene 4,** is interrupted by the appearance of what the stage directions and Macbeth refer to as Banquo's ghost. Since none of the guests can see the ghost, it remains possible that, like the dagger in Act 2, Scene 1, it is the product of Macbeth's "heat-oppressed brain." Nevertheless, this apparition terrifies Macbeth so deeply that he is unable to contain himself. Lady Macbeth tries to smooth over his outbursts and maintain decorum, but finally she has to dismiss the guests. The failure of this ceremonial feast symbolizes the complete breakdown of governmental normalcy, and from this moment on Macbeth becomes a full-fledged tyrant.

Upon learning that Macduff has refused a royal invitation, Macbeth vows to have him killed as well. He decides to visit the witches once again, and promises to continue on his program of political murders since, as he puts it, "I am in blood / Stepp'd in so far, that, should I wade no more, / Returning were as tedious as go o'er." The description of murder as tedious is a remarkable indicator of how jaded Macbeth has become, and of how meaningless human life is to him at this point. One might argue that the recognition of his own mortality has made human life, and all of its endeavors, seem finally meaningless to Macbeth. In the two brief scenes that comprise the remainder of Act 3, we learn first that the witches are preparing for Macbeth's visit (**3.5**), and then that Malcolm has been welcomed by the English King Edward, and finally that Macduff has gone there to raise support to oppose Macbeth (**3.6**).

In **Act 4, Scene 1,** Macbeth encounters the witches once again and commands them to answer his questions. They promise to give him satisfaction, and they show him three visions arising from a cauldron. First, an armed head appears and warns Macbeth to beware of Macduff, the Thane of Fife.

Then a bloody child appears from out of the cauldron and promises that "none of women born / Shall harm Macbeth." Finally, a crowned child appears with a tree in his hand and promises that Macbeth will never be defeated until the trees of Birnam wood move to Dunsinane hill outside of Macbeth's castle.

These prophecies comfort Macbeth, for he takes them to mean that he will live out the natural span of his life unconquered. Nevertheless, his thoughts still turn to Fleance, and he asks once more if Banquo's heirs will rule. In response to this request, the cauldron sinks into the earth, and a vision appears of a line of kings stretching "to th' crack of doom." The vision confirms Macbeth's worst fears, for he is told that these kings are Banquo's descendants. The witches disappear, leaving Macbeth to his thoughts, which are in turn interrupted by the arrival of Lennox with news that Macduff has fled to England.

Upset both by the witches and by the escape of Macduff, Macbeth vows never again to hesitate before fulfilling a violent impulse. Willing himself to become an unthinking killer, he decides immediately to have Macduff's family put to the sword. **Act 4, Scene 2,** sees Macbeth's murderous will put into execution. Lady Macduff and her son, left unprotected when Macduff fled to England, are brutally killed.

Meanwhile, in England, Macduff has joined Malcolm (**4.3**). The latter, wary of Macbeth's spies, tests Macduff's patriotism by declaring himself unfit to rule and attributing to himself a number of terrible vices. Macduff is horrified by Malcolm's account of himself and declares that Malcolm is not fit to rule Scotland after all. Macduff's disapproval demonstrates a true interest in the welfare of Scotland, so Malcolm decides to trust him. Disavowing all of his professed faults, Malcolm reveals that he has the support of the English king, and that an army of ten thousand soldiers has been organized to attack Macbeth.

At this point—to emphasize the righteousness of the English king and, by extension, of Malcolm's cause—a doctor enters and announces that King Edward of England is about to perform a ceremony in which he will cure his subjects by touching them and channeling to them his heavenly grace. On the one hand, such ceremonial healing is a normal part of the offices of kingship: even in Shakespeare's time it was believed by some that the touch of a legitimate king could cure scrofula. On the other hand, this extraneous reminder of the special relationship between king and God underscores both the magnitude of Macbeth's crime and the distinction between a legitimate king like Edward and a tyrant like Macbeth. As if to make the distinction clearer still, Rosse enters with news of the slaughter of Macduff's family: where a good king heals his subjects, a tyrant kills them. Choked with grief, Macduff vows to avenge the murders.

The **fifth** and final **act** of *Macbeth* begins within Macbeth's castle, as a doctor and gentlewoman look after Lady Macbeth, who has begun to display signs of nervous hysteria. As they discuss Lady Macbeth's symptoms, she herself enters sleepwalking, rubbing her hands as if to wash them, and uttering the fragmentary expressions of her guilty conscience ("Here's the smell of blood still: all the perfumes of Arabia will not sweeten this little hand"). Lady Macbeth's distraction here is reminiscent of Macbeth's stunned reaction to the murder of Duncan in Act 2, Scene 2 ("Will all great Neptune's ocean wash this blood / Clean from my hand?"), and in fact the emotional trajectories of the two characters are mirror images of one another. At the start of Act 2, Macbeth was conscience stricken while his wife was aggressive and murderous. As Macbeth becomes a jaded killer, Lady Macbeth falls prey to her conscience, with the result that by the beginning of Act 5 their roles are more or less reversed.

The **next five scenes** show preparations for war on both sides. One of the witches' prophesies is fulfilled here, as the English army cuts trees in Birnam wood and carries them aloft to Dunsinane in order to make it difficult for Macbeth to calculate the number of approaching soldiers (**5.4**). In **Act 5, Scene 5,** Macbeth's armor-bearer Seyton (a Scottish family name, but indistinguishable from "Satan" to a theater audience) brings news to Macbeth of his wife's death. The news provokes a brief, powerful meditation on the sheer meaninglessness of human actions, a meditation which boils down into a few lines the accumulated cynicism of the play:

Life's but a walking shadow; a poor player,
That struts and frets his hour upon the stage,
And then is heard no more: it is a tale
Told by an idiot, full of sound and fury,
Signifying nothing.

As the end of the play approaches, Macbeth is faced with the realization that all his power has amounted to nothing: what good is it to be king if life is so fleeting and trivial? On the heels of this speech, Macbeth is informed by a messenger that Birnam wood seems to be moving toward Dunsinane. The tyrant recognizes that this means he will be defeated, and he seems wearily to welcome death.

The battle is finally joined in **Act 5, Scene 7,** and we see Macbeth kill Young Siward, the son of the commander of the English army. In **Scene 8,** Macbeth and Macduff come face to face at last. When Macbeth boasts that no man born of a woman can hurt him, Macduff replies that he himself was a cesarean birth—"from his mother's womb / Untimely ripp'd"—and is therefore proof against Macbeth's charm. Macbeth is momentarily "cow'd" by this revelation, but the two fight on until—at last—Macduff kills the tyrant and avenges his family's slaughter.

The play's **final scene** stages the aftermath of the battle. Siward refuses to mourn the death of his son, saying that since the boy died honorably in battle, he died well and need not be lamented. The triumphant Macduff enters carrying Macbeth's severed head, and the assembled warriors all hail Malcolm as the new King of Scotland. Well pleased, Malcolm alters the honorific title of his Scottish nobles from "Thane" to "Earl" in imitation of his English allies. As the play comes to a close, Malcolm thanks his soldiers and promises to reward their service with a liberal hand.

It is tempting, and certainly appropriate, to see *Macbeth* as a study of the progressive degeneration of Macbeth's moral character as he gives free reign to his ambition. For, as Macbeth gives in to his ambition, personal desire replaces the traditional values of honor and duty as the basis for his actions. A growing awareness of the brevity and triviality of human existence, however, makes personal desire seem increasingly meaningless to Macbeth. As his actions grow worse and worse, he becomes increasingly disinterested, increasingly sure that human actions signify nothing. At the beginning of the play Macbeth is a contented and well-respected soldier, but he becomes, over the course of the play, first a reluctant regicide, then a restless and discontented king, and finally a benumbed and murderous tyrant. Seen in this way, the character becomes a study in the development of personal and political evil, and an example of what not to do. This interpretation sees Macbeth's murderous career as an aberration in a generally stable and effective social system.

However, though the play ends happily, there are several reasons to foresee further trouble for Malcolm and his subjects. For one thing, the witches are still at large, and there is no reason to think that the disorderly force they represent will not re-emerge. For another thing, Malcolm's situation at the conclusion of the play is disturbingly reminiscent of Duncan's situation at the end of its second scene. Macbeth slew Macdonwald in order to restore social order and protect Duncan; Macduff slew Macbeth in order to restore the social order and protect Malcolm's right to the throne. Especially with the witches still at large, why should we have any confidence in, for example, Macduff? Finally, the play leaves us wondering how exactly Banquo's heirs will take the throne. Since we know for a fact that Malcolm's line will be interrupted, why should we believe that the accession of Malcolm at the end of *Macbeth* ushers in an era of social stability?

An interpretation of *Macbeth* emphasizing the instability of Malcolm's rule and the continued presence of the witches might see Macbeth's tyranny not as an aberration in a healthy state, but rather as an inevitable symptom of an unhealthy one. Such a reading might find the play's tragedy not in the evil character of Macbeth but in the fact that even the benevolent government of a Duncan or a Malcolm cannot suffice to guarantee order in a world dominated by witches, tempests, and the treasonous imaginings of insuppressible ambition. ❖

—*Curtis Perry*
Harvard University

List of Characters

Macbeth is the pivotal character of the play that bears his name. At the start of the play he is a military hero, universally honored for his bravery in battle. Once the witches' promise him the crown, he can no longer silence the voice of his ambition, which leads him first to regicide and from thence to a number of unforgivable, brutal murders. Macbeth's continuing articulations of his own unique psychological turmoil are the backbone of the play. He is the only character in the play whose inner life is revealed in any depth. Consequently, despite the repugnance of his moral failings, he sustains an audience's interest, and perhaps even its sympathy, until his death in the final act.

Lady Macbeth is Macbeth's wife. She is also his advisor during his rise to power in the first half of the play. In addition to encouraging Macbeth's troubled ambition, Lady Macbeth plans the murder of Duncan, frames Duncan's servants for the murder, and keeps up appearances when the murder is discovered. In the time leading up to Duncan's murder she is presented as willful, crafty, and terrifyingly violent. In order to steel herself for the murder of Duncan, Lady Macbeth attempts to unsex herself—to banish womanly softness and replace it with a masculine spirit of aggression. She also goads Macbeth to action by repeatedly questioning his manhood. As Macbeth becomes increasingly violent during the second half of the play, Lady Macbeth recedes. By the beginning of the final act she is debilitated by her conscience, and her death shortly thereafter is almost an afterthought.

The witches, or Weird Sisters, are three "wither'd," bearded women who, under the loose direction of the goddess Hecate, preside over the world of *Macbeth.* Their prophesy galvanizes Macbeth's ambition, and their other oracular pronouncements encourage his slide into tyranny. The extent of their power is unclear, but they are associated throughout the play with the uncontrollable disorder that besets human affairs. They speak in incantatory, rhyming verse, and are always accompanied by claps of thunder. Their conversations show that they take delight in their ability to mislead human affairs, and they combine an almost comic sense of mischievousness with a frightening, violent aggressiveness.

Duncan is the Scottish king murdered by Macbeth. He is presented, in the public, ceremonial scenes in which he appears, as a generous, loving, and nurturing king. His death occasions a terrible storm and an earthquake and is described by many of the play's other characters as sacrilegious and unnatural.

Malcolm is Duncan's eldest son. When his father is killed, Malcolm flees to England in fear for his own life. There he is welcomed and supported by the English king. Malcolm carefully tests Macduff's loyalty when the latter joins him in England. In doing so, Malcolm displays the kind of political savvy that he will need as the ruler of a troubled nation. With the support of Macduff and an English army, Malcolm defeats Macbeth and is triumphantly restored to the throne.

Macduff, like Macbeth, is one of Duncan's generals. It is he who discovers Duncan's murdered body, and it is he who first openly rebels against the tyrant Macbeth. Pursuing Malcolm to England, Macduff joins forces with the exiled prince against Macbeth. While he is in England, Macduff's wife and son are killed by Macbeth's assassins. When news of this senseless slaughter reaches Macduff, he vows to take vengeance. In the play's final battle, Macduff fulfills his vow, killing Macbeth; as a cesarean birth, Macduff is able to kill Macbeth despite the promise of the witches that no man "of women born" can do him harm. Macduff is generally represented as a valiant and upstanding soldier throughout the play, though it is his decision to go to England that leaves his family vulnerable to Macbeth's murderers. In that scene, Lady Macduff bitterly criticizes her husband for leaving them alone. Since her fears turn out to be justified, one wonders if he has perhaps erred in putting his duty to Scotland before his duty to his family.

Banquo is Macbeth's fellow general in Duncan's army. He is traveling with Macbeth when the witches make their first prophecy. The witches foresee that though Banquo himself will never be a king, his descendants will rule. After meeting the witches, Banquo is troubled by disturbing thoughts which keep him up at night. Nevertheless, he is always able to maintain his sense of duty and allegiance to Duncan. Once Macbeth becomes king, he develops a fierce antipathy to Banquo. On the one hand, Banquo poses a real danger to the new king, since his firsthand knowledge of the witches' promises make him likely to suspect Macbeth's involvement in Duncan's murder. On the other hand, Macbeth is suddenly and inexplicably bothered by the idea that Banquo's line should rule in the future. Macbeth hires two murderers, who ambush Banquo and his son Fleance as they go riding. Banquo is killed and Fleance escapes. Banquo's ghost—or Macbeth's hallucination of Banquo's ghost—returns to ruin a state banquet and terrify the tyrant Macbeth.

Fleance is Banquo's son and heir. Though he is not a major player in the actions of *Macbeth,* his survival ensures that Banquo's line will persist to fulfill the witches' prophesy. When Macbeth attempts to kill Banquo and Fleance, the latter escapes. As the play ends, we do not know what has become of him. Since we do know that Fleance or his sons will eventually assume the throne of Scotland, this is an important loose end. How can we trust the stability of Malcolm's reign with Fleance at large? ✤

Critical Views

SAMUEL JOHNSON ON THE FLAWS AND VIRTUES OF *MACBETH*

[Samuel Johnson (1709–1784), perhaps the greatest British literary figure of the eighteenth century, was a poet, novelist, critic, and biographer of distinction. In 1765 he wrote a monograph, *Preface to His Edition of Shakespeare,* and in that same year he edited a landmark annotated edition of Shakespeare's works, still highly regarded for the astuteness of its commentary. In this extract, taken from the notes to his edition, Johnson offers both praise and criticism of the play.]

This play is deservedly celebrated for the propriety of its fictions, and solemnity, grandeur, and variety of its action; but it has no nice discriminations of character, the events are too great to admit the influence of particular dispositions, and the course of the action necessarily determines the conduct of the agents.

The danger of ambition is well described; and I know not whether it may not be said in defence of some parts which now seem improbable, that, in Shakespeare's time, it was necessary to warn credulity against vain and illusive predictions.

The passions are directed to their true end. Lady Macbeth is merely detested; and though the courage of Macbeth preserves some esteem, yet every reader rejoices at his fall.

> —Samuel Johnson, *The Plays of William Shakespeare* (London: J. & R. Tonson, 1765), Vol. 6, p. 484

WILLIAM HAZLITT ON MACBETH AND RICHARD III

[William Hazlitt (1778–1830) was one of the leading British essayists of the early nineteenth century. Among his many works are *Lectures on the English Poets*

(1818), *Lectures on the English Comic Writers* (1819), *The Spirit of the Age* (1825), and a moving account of his love affair with a prostitute, *Liber Amoris* (1823). In his important treatise, *Characters of Shakespear's Plays* (1817), Hazlitt begins the critical method of treating the characters of Shakespeare as if they were real individuals, a tendency that culminates in the work of A. C. Bradley. In this extract from that work, Hazlitt compares the characters of Macbeth and Richard III, claiming that Macbeth was a good man who has been corrupted by circumstances while Richard III was an evil man from the start.]

This tragedy is alike distinguished for the lofty imagination it displays, and for the tumultuous vehemence of the action; and the one is made the moving principle of the other. The overwhelming pressure of preternatural agency urges on the tide of human passion with redoubled force. Macbeth himself appears driven along by the violence of his fate like a vessel drifting before a storm: he reels to and fro like a drunken man; he staggers under the weight of his own purposes and the suggestions of others; he stands at bay with his situation; and from the superstitious awe and breathless suspense into which the communications of the Weïrd Sisters throw him, is hurried on with daring impatience to verify their predictions, and with impious and bloody hand to tear aside the veil which hides the uncertainty of the future. He is not equal to the struggle with fate and conscience. He now 'bends up each corporal instrument to the terrible feat'; at other times his heart misgives him, and he is cowed and abashed by his success. 'The deed, no less than the attempt, confounds him.' His mind is assailed by the stings of remorse, and full of 'preternatural solicitings.' His speeches and soliloquies are dark riddles on human life, baffling solution, and entangling him in their labyrinths. In thought he is absent and perplexed, sudden and desperate in act, from a distrust of his own resolution. His energy springs from the anxiety and agitation of his mind. His blindly rushing forward on the objects of his ambition and revenge, or his recoiling from them, equally betrays the harassed state of his feelings.⟨. . .⟩

The leading features in the character of Macbeth are striking enough, and they form what may be thought at first only a bold, rude, Gothic outline. By comparing it with other characters of the same author we shall perceive the absolute truth and identity which is observed in the midst of the giddy whirl and rapid career of events. Macbeth in Shakespear no more loses his identity of character in the fluctuations of fortune or the storm of passion, than Macbeth in himself would have lost the identity of his person. Thus he is as distinct a being from Richard III as it is possible to imagine, though these two characters in common hands, and indeed in the hands of any other poet, would have been a repetition of the same general idea, more or less exaggerated. For both are tyrants, usurpers, murderers, both aspiring and ambitious, both courageous, cruel, treacherous. But Richard is cruel from nature and constitution. Macbeth becomes so from accidental circumstances. Richard is from his birth deformed in body and mind, and naturally incapable of good. Macbeth is full of 'the milk of human kindness,' is frank, sociable, generous. He is tempted to the commission of guilt by golden opportunities, by the instigations of his wife, and by prophetic warnings. Fate and metaphysical aid conspire against his virtue and his loyalty. Richard on the contrary needs no prompter, but wades through a series of crimes to the height of his ambition from the ungovernable violence of his temper and a reckless love of mischief. He is never gay but in the prospect or in the success of his villainies: Macbeth is full of horror at the thoughts of the murder of Duncan, which he is with difficulty prevailed on to commit, and of remorse after its perpetration. Richard has no mixture of common humanity in his composition, no regard to kindred or posterity, he owns no fellowship with others, he is 'himself alone.' Macbeth is not destitute of feelings of sympathy, is accessible to pity, is even made in some measure the dupe of his uxoriousness, ranks the loss of friends, of the cordial love of his followers, and of his good name, among the causes which have made him weary of life, and regrets that he has ever seized the crown by unjust means, since he cannot transmit it to his posterity—

> For Banquo's issue have I fil'd my mind—
> For them the gracious Duncan have I murther'd,
> To make them kings, the seed of Banquo kings.

In the agitation of his mind, he envies those whom he has sent to peace. 'Duncan is in his grave; after life's fitful fever he sleeps well.'—It is true, he becomes more callous as he plunges deeper in guilt, 'direness is thus rendered familiar to his slaughterous thoughts,' and he in the end anticipates his wife in the boldness and bloodiness of his enterprises, while she for want of the same stimulus of action, 'is troubled with thick-coming fancies that rob her of her rest,' goes mad and dies. Macbeth endeavours to escape from reflection on his crimes by repelling their consequences, and banishes remorse for the past by the meditation of future mischief. This is not the principle of Richard's cruelty, which displays the wanton malice of a fiend as much as the frailty of human passion. Macbeth is goaded on to acts of violence and retaliation by necessity; to Richard, blood is a pastime.—There are other decisive differences inherent in the two characters. Richard may be regarded as a man of the world, a plotting, hardened knave, wholly regardless of every thing but his own ends, and the means to secure them.—Not so Macbeth. The superstitions of the age, the rude state of society, the local scenery and customs, all give a wildness and imaginary grandeur to his character. From the strangeness of the events that surround him, he is full of amazement and fear; and stands in doubt between the world of reality and the world of fancy. He sees sights not shown to mortal eye, and hears unearthly music. All is tumult and disorder within and without his mind; his purposes recoil upon himself, are broken and disjointed; he is the double thrall of his passions and his evil destiny. Richard is not a character either of imagination or pathos, but of pure self-will. There is no conflict of opposite feelings in his breast. The apparitions which he sees only haunt him in his sleep; nor does he live like Macbeth in a waking dream. Macbeth has considerable energy and manliness of character; but then he is 'subject to all the skyey influences.' He is sure of nothing but the present moment. Richard in the busy turbulence of his projects never loses his self-possession, and makes use of every circumstance that happens as an instrument of his long-reaching designs. In his last extremity we can only regard him as a wild beast taken in the toils: while we never entirely lose our concern for Macbeth; and he calls back all our sympathy by that fine close of thoughtful melancholy—

My way of life is fallen into the sear,
The yellow leaf; and that which should accompany old age,
As honour, troops of friends, I must not look to have;
But in their stead, curses not loud but deep,
Mouth-honour, breath, which the poor heart
Would fain deny, and dare not.

—William Hazlitt, *Characters of Shakespear's Plays* (1817; rpt.
London: Macmillan, 1925), pp. 11–12, 17–19

SAMUEL TAYLOR COLERIDGE ON *MACBETH* AND *HAMLET*

[Samuel Taylor Coleridge (1772–1834), aside from
being one of the greatest British poets of the early
nineteenth century, was also a penetrating critic. His
most famous critical work is *Biographia Literaria* (1817).
In 1819 he delivered a series of lectures on
Shakespeare, which were published posthumously in
his *Literary Remains* (1836–39). In this extract from that
work, Coleridge compares *Macbeth* with *Hamlet*, finding the former play more compact than the latter and
completely lacking in the punning and humor that
Hamlet features. He also notes that both plays open
with supernatural scenes, but that the purpose of these
scenes is very different.]

Macbeth stands in contrast throughout with *Hamlet*; in the
manner of opening more especially. In the latter, there is a
gradual ascent from the simplest forms of conversation to the
language of impassioned intellect,—yet the intellect still
remaining the seat of passion: in the former, the invocation is
at once made to the imagination and the emotions connected
therewith. Hence the movement throughout is the most rapid
of all Shakspeare's plays; and hence also, with the exception of
the disgusting passage of the Porter (Act ii. sc. 3.), which I dare
pledge myself to demonstrate to be an interpolation of the
actors, there is not, to the best of my remembrance, a single
pun or play on words in the whole drama. I have previously
given an answer to the thousand times repeated charge

against Shakspeare upon the subject of his punning, and I here merely mention the fact of the absence of any puns in *Macbeth,* as justifying a candid doubt at least, whether even in these figures of speech and fanciful modifications of language, Shakspeare may not have followed rules and principles that merit and would stand the test of philosophic examination. And hence, also, there is an entire absence of comedy, nay, even of irony and philosophic contemplation in *Macbeth,*—the play being wholly and purely tragic. For the same cause, there are no reasonings of equivocal morality, which would have required a more leisurely state and a consequently greater activity of mind;—no sophistry of self-delusion,—except only that previously to the dreadful act, Macbeth mistranslates the recoilings and ominous whispers of conscience into prudential and selfish reasonings, and, after the deed done, the terrors of remorse into fear from external dangers,—like delirious men who run away from the phantoms of their own brains, or, raised by terror to rage, stab the real object that is within their reach:—whilst Lady Macbeth merely endeavours to reconcile his and her own sinkings of heart by anticipations of the worst, and an affected bravado in confronting them. In all the rest, Macbeth's language is the grave utterance of the very heart, conscience-sick, even to the last faintings of moral death. It is the same in all the other characters. The variety arises from rage, caused ever and anon by disruption of anxious thought, and the quick transition of fear into it.

In *Hamlet* and *Macbeth* the scene opens with superstition; but, in each it is not merely different, but opposite. In the first it is connected with the best and holiest feelings; in the second with the shadowy, turbulent, and unsanctified cravings of the individual will. Nor is the purpose the same; in the one the object is to excite, whilst in the other it is to mark a mind already excited. Superstition, of one sort or another, is natural to victorious generals; the instances are too notorious to need mentioning. There is so much of chance in warfare, and such vast events are connected with the acts of a single individual,—the representative, in truth, of the efforts of myriads, and yet to the public and, doubtless, to his own feelings, the aggregate of all,—that the proper temperament for generating or receiving superstitious impressions is naturally produced.

Hope, the master element of a commanding genius, meeting with an active and combining intellect, and an imagination of just that degree of vividness which disquiets and impels the soul to try to realize its images, greatly increases the creative power of the mind; and hence the images become a satisfying world of themselves, as is the case in every poet and original philosopher:—but hope fully gratified, and yet the elementary basis of the passion remaining, becomes fear; and, indeed, the general, who must often feel, even though he may hide it from his own consciousness, how large a share chance had in his successes, may very naturally be irresolute in a new scene, where he knows that all will depend on his own act and election.

The Wierd Sisters are as true a creation of Shakspeare's, as his Ariel and Caliban,—fates, furies, and materializing witches being the elements. They are wholly different from any representation of witches in the contemporary writers, and yet presented a sufficient external resemblance to the creatures of vulgar prejudice to act immediately on the audience. Their character consists in the imaginative disconnected from the good; they are the shadowy obscure and fearfully anomalous of physical nature, the lawless of human nature,—elemental avengers without sex or kin:

> Fair is foul, and foul is fair;
> Hover thro' the fog and filthy air.

—Samuel Taylor Coleridge, "Notes on *Macbeth*" (1819), *Literary Remains*, ed. Henry Nelson Coleridge (London: William Pickering, 1836), Vol. 2, pp. 235–38

VICTOR HUGO ON MACBETH AS HUNGER

[Victor Hugo (1802–1885), the celebrated French novelist and author of *Notre Dame de Paris* (1831; translated into English as *The Hunchback of Notre Dame*) and *Les Misérables* (1862), wrote a book on Shakespeare in

1864. In this extract from that work, which is written in a very flamboyant and impressionistic style, Hugo maintains that the essence of Macbeth's character is not ambition so much as it is hunger and covetousness.]

To say "Macbeth is ambition," is to say nothing. Macbeth is hunger. What hunger? The hunger of the monster, always possible in man. Certain souls have teeth. Do not arouse their hunger.

To bite at the apple is a fearful thing. The apple is named "Omnia," says Filesac, that doctor of the Sorbonne who confessed Ravaillac. Macbeth has a wife whom the chronicle calls Gruoch. This Eve tempts this Adam. Once Macbeth has taken the first bite, he is lost. The first thing that Adam produces with Eve is Cain; the first thing that Macbeth accomplishes with Gruoch is murder.

Covetousness easily becoming violence, violence easily becoming crime, crime easily becoming madness: this progression is in Macbeth. Covetousness, Crime, Madness—these three night-hags have spoken to him in the solitude, and have invited him to the throne. The cat Gray-malkin has called him: Macbeth will be cunning; the toad Paddock has called him: Macbeth will be horror. The unsexed being, Gruoch, completes him. It is done; Macbeth is no longer a man. He is no longer anything but an unconscious energy rushing wildly toward evil. Henceforth, no notion of right; appetite is everything. The transitory right of royalty, the eternal right of hospitality—Macbeth murders both. He does more than slay them: he ignores them. Before they fell bleeding under his hand, they already lay dead within his soul. Macbeth begins by this parricide,—the murder of Duncan, his guest; a crime so terrible that, as a consequence, in the night when their master is stabbed, the horses of Duncan become wild again. The first step taken, the ground begins to crumble; it is the avalanche. Macbeth rolls headlong; he is precipitated; he falls and rebounds from one crime to another, ever deeper and deeper. He undergoes the mournful gravitation of matter invading the soul. He is a thing that destroys. He is a stone of ruin, a flame of war, a beast of prey, a scourge. He marches over all Scotland, king as he is, his barelegged kernes and his heavily armed gallow–glasses slaughtering, pillaging, massacring. He decimates the thanes, he murders Banquo, he murders all the Macduffs except the one that shall slay him, he murders the nobility, he murders the people, he murders his country, he murders "sleep." At length the catastrophe arrives,—the forest of Birnam moves against him. Macbeth has infringed all, overstepped all, destroyed all, violated all; and this desperation ends in arousing even Nature. Nature loses patience, Nature enters into action against Macbeth, Nature becomes soul against the man who has become brute force.

This drama has epic proportions. Macbeth represents that frightful hungry creature who prowls throughout history—in the forest called brigand, and on the throne, conqueror. The ancestor of Macbeth is Nimrod. These men of force, are they forever furious? Let us be just; no. They have a goal, which being attained, they stop. Give to Alexander, to Cyrus, to Sesostris, to Caesar—what?—the world; they are appeased. Geoffrey St. Hilaire said to me one day: "When the lion has eaten, he is at peace with Nature." For Cambyses, Sennacherib, Genghis Khan, and the like, to have eaten is to possess the whole earth. They would calm themselves down in the process of digesting the human race.

> —Victor Hugo, *William Shakespeare* (1864), tr. Melville B. Anderson (Chicago: A. C. McClurg, 1887), pp. 240–42

A. C. BRADLEY ON THE USE OF PROSE IN *MACBETH*

[A. C. Bradley (1851–1935) was the leading British Shakespeare scholar of his time. He taught at the University of Liverpool, the University of Glasgow, and at Oxford University, and wrote *Oxford Lectures on Poetry* (1909) and *A Miscellany* (1929). In this extract, taken from his celebrated book, *Shakespearean Tragedy* (1904), Bradley makes the interesting observation that the prose portions of *Macbeth* and of other Shakespeare plays seem generally designed to indicate a condition of abnormality or madness on the part of the speaker.]

The speeches of the Porter, a low comic character, are in prose. So is the letter of Macbeth to his wife. In both these cases Shakespeare follows his general rule or custom. The only other prose-speeches occur in the sleep-walking scene, and here the use of prose may seem strange. For in great tragic scenes we expect the more poetic medium of expression, and this is one of the most famous of such scenes. Besides, unless I mistake, Lady Macbeth is the only one of Shakespeare's great tragic characters who on a last appearance is denied the dignity of verse.

Yet in this scene also he adheres to his custom. Somnambulism is an abnormal condition, and it is his general rule to assign prose to persons whose state of mind is abnormal. Thus, to illustrate from these four plays, Hamlet when playing the madman speaks prose, but in soliloquy, in talking with Horatio, and in pleading with his mother, he speaks verse. Ophelia in her madness either sings snatches of songs or speaks prose. Almost all Lear's speeches, after he has become definitely insane, are in prose: where he wakes from sleep recovered, the verse returns. The prose enters with that speech which closes with his trying to tear off his clothes; but he speaks in verse—some of it very irregular—in the Timon-like speeches where his intellect suddenly in his madness seems to regain the force of his best days (IV. vi.). Othello, in IV. i., speaks in verse till the moment when Iago tells him that Cassio has confessed. There follow ten lines of prose—exclamations and mutterings of bewildered horror—and he falls to the ground unconscious.

The idea underlying this custom of Shakespeare's evidently is that the regular rhythm of verse would be inappropriate where the mind is supposed to have lost its balance and to be at the mercy of chance impressions coming from without (as sometimes with Lear), or of ideas emerging from its unconscious depths and pursuing one another across its passive surface. The somnambulism of Lady Macbeth is such a condition. There is no rational connection in the sequence of images and ideas. The sight of blood on her hand, the sound of the clock striking the hour for Duncan's murder, the hesitation of her husband before that hour came, the vision of the old man in his blood, the idea of the murdered wife of Macduff, the sight of the hand again, Macbeth's 'flaws and starts' at the sight of Banquo's ghost, the smell on her hand, the washing of hands after Duncan's murder again, her husband's fear of the buried Banquo, the sound of the knocking at the gate—these possess her, one after another, in this chance order. It is not much less accidental than the order of Ophelia's ideas; the great difference is that with Ophelia total insanity has effaced or greatly weakened the emotional force of the ideas, whereas to Lady Macbeth each new image or perception comes laden with anguish. There is, again, scarcely a sign of the exaltation of disordered imagination; we are conscious rather of an intense suffering which forces its way into light against resistance, and speaks a language for the most part strikingly bare in its diction and simple in its construction. This language stands in strong contrast with that of Macbeth in the surrounding scenes, full of a feverish and almost furious excitement, and seems to express a far more desolating misery.

The effect is extraordinarily impressive. The soaring pride and power of Lady Macbeth's first speeches return on our memory, and the change is felt with a breathless awe. Any attempt, even by Shakespeare, to draw out the moral enfolded in this awe, would but weaken it. For the moment, too, all the language of poetry—even of Macbeth's poetry—seems to be touched with unreality, and these brief toneless sentences seem the only voice of truth.

—A. C. Bradley, *Shakespearean Tragedy* (London: Macmillan, 1904), pp. 397–400

SIGMUND FREUD ON MACBETH AS PARRICIDE

[Sigmund Freud (1856–1939) is the German psychologist who founded psychoanalysis. Among his most important books translated into English are *The Interpretation of Dreams* (1913) and *A General*

Introduction to Psychoanalysis (1920). Freud frequently devoted his attention to the study of literature from a psychoanalytic perspective. In this extract, Freud sees Macbeth's murder of Duncan as a kind of parricide (killing of the father) related to Macbeth's fervent desire for offspring so as to continue his dynasty.]

Shakespeare's *Macbeth* is a *pièce d'occasion*, written for the accession of James, who had hitherto been King of Scotland. The plot was ready-made, and had been handled by other contemporary writers, whose work Shakespeare probably made use of in his customary manner. It offered remarkable analogies to the actual situation. The 'virginal' Elizabeth, of whom it was rumoured that she had never been capable of childbearing and who had once described herself as 'a barren stock', in an anguished outcry at the news of James's birth, was obliged by this very childlessness of hers to let the Scottish king become her successor. And he was the son of that Mary Stuart whose execution she, though reluctantly, had decreed, and who, despite the clouding of their relations by political concerns, was yet of her blood and might be called her guest.

The accession of James I. was like a demonstration of the curse of unfruitfulness and the blessings reserved for those who carry on the race. And Shakespeare's *Macbeth* develops on the theme of this same contrast. The three Fates, the 'weird sisters', have assured him that he shall indeed be king, but to Banquo they promise that *his* children shall obtain possession of the crown. Macbeth is incensed by this decree of destiny; he is not content with the satisfaction of his own ambition, he desires to found a dynasty and not to have murdered for the benefit of strangers. This point is overlooked when Shakespeare's play is regarded only as a tragedy of ambition. It is clear that Macbeth cannot live for ever, and thus there is but one way for him to disprove that part of the prophecy which opposes his wishes—namely, to have children himself, children who can succeed him. And he seems to expect them from his vigorous wife:

> Bring forth men-children only!
> For thy undaunted mettle should compose
> Nothing but males. . . .   (Act I. Sc. 7.)

And equally it is clear that if he is deceived in this expectation he must submit to destiny; otherwise his actions lose all purpose and are transformed into the blind fury of one doomed to destruction, who is resolved to destroy beforehand all that he can reach. We watch Macbeth undergo this development, and at the height of the tragedy we hear that shattering cry from Macduff, which has often ere now been recognized to have many meanings and possibly to contain the key to the change in Macbeth:

> He has no children! (Act IV. Sc. 3.)

Undoubtedly that signifies 'Only because he is himself childless could he murder my children'; but more may be implied in it, and above all it might be said to lay bare the essential motive which not only forces Macbeth to go far beyond his own true nature, but also assails the hard character of his wife at its only weak place. If one looks back upon *Macbeth* from the culmination reached in these words of Macduff's, one sees that the whole play is sown with references to the father-and-children relation. The murder of the kindly Duncan is little else than parricide; in Banquo's case, Macbeth kills the father while the son escapes him; and he kills Macduff's children because the father has fled from him. A bloody child, and then a crowned one, are shown him by the witches in the conjuration-scene; the armed head seen previously is doubtless Macbeth's own. But in the background arises the sinister form of the avenger, Macduff, who is himself an exception to the laws of generation, since he was not born of his mother but ripp'd from her womb.

—Sigmund Freud, "Some Character-Types Met With in Psycho-Analytic Work" (1915), *Collected Papers*, tr. Joan Riviere (New York: Basic Books, 1959), Vol. 4, pp. 328–30

G. Wilson Knight on Fear, Evil, and Nightmare in *Macbeth*

[G. Wilson Knight (1897–1939), a leading British Shakespeare scholar, taught drama and English literature at the University of Leeds. He was the author of many volumes of criticism, including *The Starlit Dome* (1941), *The Crown of Life* (1947), and *Shakespeare and Religion* (1967). In this extract, taken from an essay in his early and important volume, *The Wheel of Fire* (1930), Knight believes that it is fear that drives Macbeth to commit his evil acts, thereby thrusting him into a world of nightmare and unreality.]

The central human theme—the temptation and crime of Macbeth—is ⟨. . .⟩ easy of analysis. The crucial speech runs as follows:

> Why do I yield to that suggestion,
> Whose horrid image doth unfix my hair,
> And makes my seated heart knock at my ribs
> Against the use of nature? Present fears
> Are less than horrible imaginings.
> My thought whose murder yet is but fantastical
> Shakes so my single state of man that function
> Is smother'd in surmise, and nothing is
> But what is not.
>
> (I. iii. 134)

These lines, spoken when Macbeth first feels the impending evil, expresses again all those elements I have noticed in the mass-effect of the play: questioning doubt, horror, fear of some unknown power; horrible imaginings of the supernatural and 'fantastical'; an abysm of unreality; disorder on the plane of physical life. This speech is a microcosm of the *Macbeth* vision: it contains the germ of the whole. Like a stone in a pond, this original immediate experience of Macbeth sends ripples of itself expanding over the whole play. This is the moment of the birth of evil in *Macbeth*—he may have had ambitious thoughts before, may even have intended the murder, but now for the first time he feels its oncoming reality. This is the mental experience which he projects into action, thereby plunging his land, too, in fear, horror, darkness, and disorder. In this speech we have a swift interpenetration of idea with idea, from fear and disorder, through sickly imaginings, to abysmal darkness, nothingness. 'Nothing is but what is not': that is the text of the play. Reality and unreality change places. We must see that Macbeth, like the whole universe of this play, is paralysed, mesmerized, as though in a dream. This is not merely 'ambition'—it is fear, a nameless fear which yet fixes itself to a horrid image. He is helpless as a man in a nightmare: and this helplessness is integral to the conception—the will-concept is absent. Macbeth may struggle, but he cannot fight: he can no more resist than a rabbit resists a weasel's teeth fastened in its neck, or a bird the serpent's transfixing eye. Now this evil in Macbeth propels him to an act absolutely evil. For, though no ethical system is ultimate, Macbeth's crime is as near absolute as may be. It is therefore conceived as absolute. Its dastardly nature is emphasized clearly (I. vii. 12–25): Duncan is old, good; he is at once Macbeth's kinsman, king, and guest; he is to be murdered in sleep. No worse act of evil could well be found. So the evil of which Macbeth is at first aware rapidly entraps him in a mesh of events: it makes a tool of Duncan's visit, it dominates Lady Macbeth. It is significant that she, like her husband, is influenced by the Weird Sisters and their prophecy. Eventually Macbeth undertakes the murder, as a grim and hideous duty. He cuts a sorry figure at first, but, once embarked on his allegiant enterprise of evil, his grandeur grows. Throughout he is driven by fear—the fear that paralyses everyone else urges him to an amazing and mysterious action of blood. This action he repeats, again and again.

By his original murder he isolates himself from humanity. He is lonely, endures the uttermost torture of isolation. Yet still a bond unites him to men: that bond he would 'cancel and tear to pieces'—the natural bond of human fellowship and love. He further symbolizes his guilty, pariah soul by murdering Banquo. He fears everyone outside himself but his wife, suspects them. Every act of blood is driven by fear of the horrible disharmony existent between himself and his world. He tries to harmonize the relation by murder. He would let 'the frame of things disjoint, both the worlds suffer' (III. ii. 16) to win back peace. He is living in an unreal world, a fantastic mockery, a ghoulish dream: he strives to make his single nightmare to rule the outward things of his nation. He would make all Scotland a nightmare thing of dripping blood. He knows he cannot return, so determines to go o'er. He seeks out the Weird Sisters a second time. Now he welcomes disorder and confusion, would let them range wide over the earth, since they range unfettered in his own soul:

> . . . though the treasure
> Of nature's germens tumble all together,
> Even till destruction sicken; answer me
> To what I ask you. (IV. i. 58)

So he addresses the Weird Sisters. Castles, palaces, and pyramids—let all fall in general confusion, if only Macbeth be satisfied. He is plunging deeper and deeper into unreality, the severance from mankind and all normal forms of life is now abysmal, deep. Now he is shown Apparitions glassing the future. They promise him success in terms of natural law; no man 'of woman born' shall hurt him, he shall not be vanquished till Birnam Wood come against him. He, based firmly in the unreal, yet thinks to build his future on the laws of reality. He forgets that he is trafficking with things of nightmare fantasy, whose truth is falsehood, falsehood truth. That success they promise is unreal as they themselves. So, once having cancelled the bond of reality he has no home: the unreal he understands not, the real condemns him. In neither can he exist. He asks if Banquo's issue shall reign in Scotland: most horrible thought to him, since, if that be so, it proves that the future takes its natural course irrespective of human acts—that prophecy need not have been interpreted into crime: that he would in truth have been King of Scotland without his own 'stir' (I. iii. 144). Also the very thought of other succeeding and prosperous kings, some of them with 'twofold balls and treble sceptres' (IV. i. 121), is a maddening thing to him who is no real king but only monarch of a nightmare realm. The Weird Sisters who were formerly as the three Parcae, or Fates, foretelling Macbeth's future, now, at this later stage of his story, become the Erinyes, avengers of murder, symbols of the tormented soul. They delude and madden him with their apparitions and ghosts. Yet he does not give way, and raises our admiration at his undaunted severance from good. He contends for his own individual soul against the universal reality. Nor is his nightmare fear of his life—he goes on 'till destruction sicken' (IV. i. 60): he actually does 'go o'er'—is not lost in the stream of blood he elects to cross. It is true. He wins his battle.

He adds crime to crime and emerges at last victorious and fear-less:

> I have almost forgot the taste of fears:
> The time has been, my senses would have cool'd
> To hear a night-shriek; and my fell of hair
> Would at a dismal treatise rouse and stir
> As life were in't; I have supp'd full with horrors;
> Direness, familiar to my slaughterous thoughts,
> Cannot once start me.   (V. v. 9)

Again, 'Hang those that talk of fear!' (V. iii. 36) he cries, in an ecstasy of courage. He is, at last, 'broad and general as the cas-ing air' (III. iv. 23).

—G. Wilson Knight, "Macbeth and the Metaphysics of Evil," *The Wheel of Fire* (1930; 4th rev. ed. London: Methuen, 1949), pp. 152–56

M. C. BRADBROOK ON THE SOURCES FOR *MACBETH*

[Muriel Clara Bradbrook (1909–1993) was an important British Shakespeare scholar, and a professor of English and former principal of Girton College, Cambridge. Among her many works are *Themes and Conventions of Elizabethan Tragedy* (1935; rev. ed. 1980) and *The Rise of the Common Player* (1962). Her *Collected Papers* (mostly on Shakespeare) appeared in four volumes in 1982 and 1989. In this extract, Bradbrook studies the sources for *Macbeth* in Raphael Holinshed's *Chronicles* (1577), finding that Shakespeare has greatly elaborated upon Holinshed's very brief and skeletonic account.]

In reading through Holinshed's voluminous Scottish Chronicles, Shakespeare would come, about a third of the way through, upon the story of Duncan, the eighty-fourth king according to that account, and the narrative with which we are all familiar. The chronicle gives a brief and bald summary of reign after reign, describing the same round of violence, murder, rebellion and general turbulence. It is as monotonous as the series of apocryphal portraits of these early kings to be seen in Holyrood Palace; and the power of its monotony is considerable. The picture of a strange, bleak, haunted world emerges, where savage beings fulfil the passionate cycle of their dreadful lives as if under enchanted compulsion. But why, in reading through these legendary stories, did Shakespeare stop where he did?

The story of Duncan and Macbeth glorified the ancestors of King James, both the ancient house of Macalpine, and in Banquo, an imaginary figure invented by Hector Boece during the fifteenth century, the later Stewart line. It also introduced the weird sisters, whose prophecies might be adapted to foretell the happy future rule of King James himself, and who were at the same time akin to the North Berwick witches whose practices against him had provided one of the most celebrated witch-trials of the age. Moreover, Malcolm Canmore, husband of the English princess Margaret and initiator of many new customs, stood at the beginning of one new age in Scottish history, as James, heir to the united crowns of Scotland and England, stood at the beginning of another. A royal command performance was clearly in view from the very inception of the play.

In the Chronicle, the history of Macbeth is briefly told, but Shakespeare shaped it both by expansion and compression. He crammed into a single act of war the rebellion of Macdonwald, two Danish invasions and the revolt of Cawdor—which happened only *after* the prophecy in Holinshed. The whole account of how Duncan was murdered he took from elsewhere, the murder of King Duff; though Macbeth's stratagem to send into the Danish camp supplies of drugged food and surprise them "so amazed that they were unable to make any defence" might have suggested the drugging of the grooms. In the Chronicle, Macbeth slew Duncan in open revolt, and no indications of remorse are given either before or after the event. The long reign of Macbeth Shakespeare shortens into a few weeks; the wizard who prophesied to Macbeth about Birnam Wood merges with the weird sisters; Macbeth's death takes place before Dunsinane, and not at the end of an inglorious flight. In sum, the debt to the Chronicle is of the slightest; so bald a narrative gave Shakespeare the merest skeleton of a plot. There is, however, one scene, that between Malcolm and Macduff in England, which is reported in very great detail. Indeed, it is out of all focus in the Chronicle and occupies almost as much space as the whole of the rest of the reign. This scene represents Shakespeare's greatest debt to Holinshed; clearly it took his eye, and here perhaps is the germ of how he first conceived the play.

—M. C. Bradbrook, "The Sources of *Macbeth*," *Shakespeare Survey* 5 (1951): 35–36

L. C. KNIGHTS ON THE VIOLATION OF NATURE IN *MACBETH*

[L. C. Knights (b. 1906), Professor Emeritus of English at Cambridge University, is a leading British critic of Shakespeare and other writers and the author of *Drama and Society in the Age of Jonson* (1937), *Explorations* (1947), *Further Explorations* (1965), *Selected Essays in Criticism* (1981), and other volumes. In this extract, from his book *Some Shakespearean Themes* (1959), Knight discusses how Macbeth violates explicitly recognized standards of human nature, thereby threatening to bring about the wild "state of nature" later described by Thomas Hobbes in *Leviathan* (1651).]

There is no vague "philosophy of nature" in *Macbeth*. The nature against which the "unnaturalness" of the Macbeth evil is defined and judged is human nature; and essential characteristics of that nature—its capacity for and intimate dependence on relationship—are powerfully evoked throughout the play. In act 3, scene 4 Macbeth, overcome by his vision of Banquo's ghost, glances back to a time when murder was common, to what will later be known as the Hobbesian state of nature.

> Blood hath been shed ere now, i' th' olden time,
> Ere humane statute purg'd the gentle weal;
> Ay, and since too, murthers have been perform'd

Too terrible for the ear: the time has been,
That, when the brains were out, the man would die,
And there an end; but now, they rise again,
With twenty mortal murthers on their crowns,
And push us from our stools. This is more strange
Than such a murther is.   (3.4.74–82)

This is a more profound version of the origins of society than is
suggested by the notion of contract or expediency. What
"purges" the supposed mere multitude and makes it into a
"gentle" commonweal is a decree greater than any law in
which it may be embodied, for it is what is dictated by the very
fact of being human; if you accept your humanity then you
can't murder with impunity. Nor is this simply a matter of judi-
cial punishment: the murdered man "rises" again, in you.
Killing may be common in wild nature, but it is not natural to
man as man; it is a violation of his essential humanity. When
Lady Macbeth describes her husband as "too full o' the milk of
human kindness" she intends to be disparaging, as Goneril
does when she speaks of Albany's "milky gentleness" or calls
him a "milk-liver'd man" (*King Lear*, 1.4.351; 4.2.50). But what
the phrase also says is that human kindness is natural to man as
man, and, like his mother's milk, nourishes his manhood. When
Malcolm accuses himself of imaginary crimes, and in so doing
reflects the evil that Macbeth has brought on Scotland, the cli-
max is,

            Nay, had I power, I should
Pour the sweet milk of concord into Hell,
Uproar the universal peace, confound
All unity in earth.   (4.3.97–100)

"Concord," "peace," "unity"—these are *active* words, signifying not a mere absence of disagreeables, a mere deliverance
from "continual fear, and danger of violent death," but the condition of positive human living. We learn little about a play by
making lists of words, but it is a significant fact that *Macbeth*
contains a very large number of words expressing the varied
relations of life (not only "cousin," "children," "servants,"
"guest," "host," but "thanks," "payment," "service," "loyalty,"
"duties"), and that these sometimes, as in act 1 scenes 4 and 6,
seem to be dwelt on with a special insistence. At the end of

the play, when Macbeth thinks of what he has lost, it is not "honour, wealth and ease in waning age" (*The Rape of Lucrece*, 1. 142) but

> that which should accompany old age,
> As honour, love, obedience, troops of friends,   (5.3.24–25)

An awareness of those "holy cords" which, though they may be severed, are "too intrince"—too intimately intertwined—"to unloose" (*King Lear*, 2.2.75–76), is integral to the imaginative structure of *Macbeth*. That the man who breaks the bonds that tie him to other men, who "pours the sweet milk of concord into Hell," is at the same time violating his own nature and thwarting his own deepest needs, is something that the play dwells on with a special insistence.

Now as we have seen in relation to *King Lear* it is only when the essential needs and characteristics of human nature are given an absolute, unconditional priority, that nature in its widest sense can be invoked as an order underlying, invigorating, and in a certain sense offering a pattern for, human nature. So too in *Macbeth*. In Macbeth's apocalyptic soliloquy before the murder, the "Pity" that dominates the chaotic natural forces and rides the whirlwind appears as a newborn babe—an offspring of humanity, naked, vulnerable, and powerful. It is, we may say, because of the symbol of the babe, and all it stands for, that Shakespeare can invoke the powers of nature and associate them, as Professor Wilson Knight shows that he does, with all that is opposed to, and finally victorious over, the powers of destruction.

> —L. C. Knights, "Macbeth: A Lust for Power," *Some Shakespearean Themes* (London: Chatto & Windus, 1959), pp. 133–35

JOHN BERRYMAN ON LADY MACBETH

[John Berryman (1914–1972) was one of the most significant American poets of his generation and author of such volumes of poetry as *The Dispossessed* (1948), *Homage to Mistress Bradstreet* (1956), and *77 Dream Songs* (1964). He also wrote a small number of critical essays, gathered in *The Freedom of the Poet* (1976). In this extract, Berryman analyzes the figure of Lady Macbeth, finding her ambitious but "short-winded"— that is, unwilling to pursue evil to its bitter end as Macbeth does.]

We might approach the characters of Lady Macbeth and Macbeth through one of her observations about him in her soliloquy (i. 5. 21–2):

> what thou wouldst highly,
> That wouldst thou holily . . .

Here is a remark unlike any ever made by an actual human being since the beginning of speech—as unlike life as a great work of music is unlike anyone's humming. Its *subject* is life, but the means is high art, *just as* the means—the true means— of "Take the Fool away" was. What is Shakespeare telling us, through Lady Macbeth, about Macbeth and about herself? Macbeth is ambitious, but an idealist. Now Lady Macbeth is ambitious also, as the whole soliloquy sufficiently shows. But the tone of contempt in "holily"—extraordinary word!—tells us that she not only possesses no such double nature herself but complains of it in him. Lady Macbeth's character—about which so much has been written—is very simple. She is unscrupulous, but short-winded. No doubts beset her, except about the steadfastness of her accomplice. Single-natured, she is even willing to lose the nature she has ("unsex me here") in order to accomplish her purpose. But, nihilistic, she has no staying power. Macbeth stays the course. By Act III she has already ceased to matter, weary, plunging toward insanity and suicide. The nature was shallow from the beginning, with its confidence that "A little water clears us of this deed"; only ambition mobilizes it, and only the horror of guilt can deepen it. There are just enough touches of sensibility—her analysis of her husband, and "Had he not resembled / My father as he slept I had done't"— to make her seem lifelike.

Lady Macbeth, in short, has no idea of what she is getting into. Now the reason she is conceived in this way, of course, is that she may throw a contrasting light on her husband, who is double-natured, heroic, uncertainly wicked, both loyal and faithless, meditative and violent, and *does* know what he is getting into. This knowledge of his is the real burden of the great soliloquy in i. 7:

> If it were done when 'tis done, then 'twere well
> It were done quickly;

The first "done" here means "finished," and the lines that follow show that what Macbeth has in mind is far deeper and more savage than any mere not-getting-away-with-the-murder, so to speak. Macbeth believes in "justice," and is afraid of teaching his own assassin (later) what to do; and he believes in eternal life, punishment, and would like to *skip* it ("jump the life to come"). He *believes*; his wife believes in nothing except her own ambition and her own guilt. He is also given to us as "brave," and "deserving" to be so called, and "worthy," and "frank," and he is full of scruples. But he has another nature. He is envious, ambitious, and hypocritical (the reasons he gives his wife, at i. 7. 31ff., for not proceeding are quite different from the reasons he has just given himself). Therefore, he can be tempted. Shakespeare holds the balance exquisitely even between supernatural *solicitation* to evil (original) and supernatural *encouragement* to evil (secondary), as in Macbeth's line to the apparitional dagger:

> Thou marshall'st me the way that I was going . . .

Holding the balance even is really to ask: does it matter? Does it matter, that is, whether man falls in with temptation or just falls? The world is certainly full of temptations, whether created by nature or by the underworld of man's nature.

This duality of Macbeth is what makes the play possible; it also accounts for the ambiguity, the mystery, that characterizes the play throughout. But it only partly accounts for his hold upon the audience's or reader's sympathy. This is primarily a response to the imagination with which his creator has endowed Macbeth. His imagination mediates between his two natures, expressing and accounting for both, and projecting itself also into the future, in a way inaccessible to Lady Macbeth. One minute before she is bleating about "A little water," he has said:

> Will all great Neptune's ocean wash this blood
> Clean from my hand? No, this my hand will rather
> The multitudinous seas incarnadine.
> Making the green one red.

His mysterious brooding has scarcely a parallel elsewhere even in Shakespeare's work. Increasingly, as the play advances, its antithetical subjects are cruelty and his own suffering; hand in hand these move, until the universe seems to consist of nothing else. There is nothing in *Macbeth* so intolerable as the last act of *Othello*, but no other Shakespearean tragedy is so desolate, and this desolation is conveyed to us through the fantastic imagination of its hero.

—John Berryman, "Notes on *Macbeth*," *The Freedom of the Poet* (New York: Farrar, Straus & Giroux, 1976), pp. 64–66

MARILYN FRENCH ON GENDER ROLES IN *MACBETH*

[Marilyn French (b. 1929) is an important feminist critic and novelist. She has written such studies as *Beyond Power: On Women, Men, and Morals* (1985) and *The War against Women* (1992), as well as such highly regarded novels as *The Women's Room* (1977) and *Our Father* (1994). She has taught at Hofstra University and the College of the Holy Cross. In this extract, French maintains that because Shakespeare to some degree accepted conventional beliefs about the respective roles of men and women, he portrays Macbeth as merely morally evil but Lady Macbeth as supernaturally evil.]

The reason ambiguity of gender is an element in the play is that Shakespeare did indeed associate certain qualities with the two genders. Perhaps he was shocked, and his imagination triggered by a passage in Holinshed describing women in Scotland fighting with hardiness, courage, and unshrinking bloodthirstiness. But he makes Macbeth's Scotland a world of what seems to be constant war, that is, a "heroic" culture. In such worlds, the felicities of life must be put aside, and procreation is tenuous: the means by which life is sustained become all important. His sense of such worlds is demonstrated in IV, iii, when Macduff tries to convince Malcolm to raise an army and oppose Macbeth. He tells Malcolm "Each new morn / New widows howl, new orphans cry." Ross alludes to depredation of the feminine principle: Scotland "cannot be called our mother, but our grave." Malcolm's presence in the country, he says, "would create new soldiers, make our women fight" (IV, iii, 165–166, 178). In "heroic" worlds, women must become as men, and the loss such a situation entails to the culture at large is the subject of the tragedy.

The world of Scotland is one of blood and brutality. Indeed, the first human words of the play are "What bloody man is that?" The answer describes the hero, Macbeth:

> Disdaining Fortune, with his brandish'd steel,
> Which smok'd with bloody execution,
> Like valor's minion carv'd out his passage
> Till he fac'd the slave;
> Which nev'r shook hands, nor bade farewell to him,
> Till he unseam'd him from the nave to th' chops,
> And fix'd his head upon our battlements.   (I, ii, 17–23)

Such a description might shock and appall an audience, might imply that the hero is not totally admirable, if not for the fact that we hear only praise for Macbeth. He is "brave Macbeth," "valor's minion," "valiant cousin," and "worthy gentleman." Most of the praise comes from Duncan, the King, the authority figure. The Sergeant's hideous description of the fighters' motivations: "Except they meant to bathe in reeking wounds, / Or memorize another Golgotha, / I cannot tell," reaps only more praise and reward.

At the conclusion of this tragedy, we accept without demur the judgment that Macbeth is a butcher. In fact, however, he is no more a butcher at the end than he is at the beginning. Macbeth lives in a culture that values butchery. Throughout the play manhood is equated with the ability to kill. Power is the highest value in Scotland, and in Scottish culture, power is military prowess. Macbeth's crime is not that he is a murderer: he is praised and rewarded for being a murderer. His crime is a failure to make the distinction his culture expects among the objects of his slaughter.

A world that maintains itself by violence must, for the sake of sanity, fence off some segment—family, the block, the neighborhood, the state—within which violence is not the proper mode of action. In this "civilized" segment of the world, law, custom, hierarchy, and tradition are supposed to supersede the right of might. Although this inner circle is no more "natural" or "unnatural" than the outer one (so far as we can judge. Some people believe that aggression is profoundly "natural" to humankind. I believe humans are basically timorous, and that aggression is forcibly taught, learned under duress. Neither position however can be proven), the play insists that the inner world is bound in accordance with a principle of nature which is equivalent to a divine law.

From the perspective of this study, the inner world is one which harmonizes the two gender principles. Ruled by law, inherited legitimacy, hierarchy, and rights of ownership, the inner world also demands a degree of subordination in all its members. Everyone, including the ruler, must relinquish some worldly power (increasingly as one goes down the social scale) in favor of the good of the whole, if felicity and an environment favorable to procreation is to exist. Those with great power must restrain it; those without power must accept their places gracefully. Without such relinquishment, felicities like friendship, ceremony, orderly succession, peaceful love, hospitality, pleasure, and even the ability to sleep at night become difficult or impossible. An essential condition of this inviolable segment of the world is that the laws bind by themselves. They are not enforceable because enforcement is part of the larger outer sphere, the violent world. If the laws of the inner world must be enforced, that world becomes identical with the outer one.

The laws therefore exist only insofar as the members of the group abide by them. Macbeth chooses to break the rules.

The factor responsible for Macbeth's doing so is Lady Macbeth. Although it is clear that Macbeth has, before the opening of the play, considered taking over the kingdom by force, it is also clear from his hesitation that he could easily be dissuaded from killing Duncan. And within the feminine/masculine polarity of morals and roles in Shakespeare's division of experience, it is Lady Macbeth's function so to dissuade him. But Lady Macbeth, a powerful person, is drawn to the role in which worldly power resides. She seems to be, by the world's standards, an exemplary wife. She encourages and supports her husband in good wifely fashion; she does not undermine him; she sees, knows, and understands the terms of the world she lives in, and she accepts them.

Yet at the end of the play, when her husband earns the attribute of "butcher," she, who has not personally performed acts of violence, is called "fiend-like." In Shakespeare's eyes, Macbeth has violated moral law; Lady Macbeth has violated natural law. Her reasoning, in urging Macbeth to the murder, is not unlike that of MacDonwald: he is called *traitor* and *slave*. Both of these terms refer to the ethical world of legitimacy: one suggests resistance to the currently constituted authority; the other insists on illegitimacy. But Lady Macbeth is not so judged; she is seen as supernaturally evil. Her crime is heinous because it violates her social role, which has been erected into a principle of experience: she fails to uphold the feminine principle. For her, as for Goneril, this failure plunges her more deeply into a pit of evil than any man can ever fall.
> —Marilyn French, *Shakespeare's Division of Experience* (New York: Summit Books, 1981), pp. 242–44

Lisa Low on Why We Are Drawn to Macbeth

[Lisa Low is a professor of English at Pace University and the author of *Milton, the Metaphysicals, and Romanticism* (1994). In this extract, Low believes that, although we perceive Macbeth to be profoundly evil, we are drawn to him because we can easily imagine ourselves to be in his position.]

Unlike most tragic heroes, Macbeth is much less sinned against than sinning, which makes him a strange candidate for our affections. He does not fall prey to infirmity like Lear, nor is he ignorant of what he does like Oedipus. He is not like Romeo, well-intentioned but too hasty; nor is he like Hamlet, Romeo's inverse, too cool. Too hot to stop, too cool to feel, Macbeth is no Romeo and no Hamlet. He is a fiend and a butcher. Standing before him, we cannot but be paralyzed with fear.

And yet, almost against our wills, we are drawn to Macbeth. We should not be, but we are. We are with him in his darkest hours and though we cannot especially hope for his success, we share with him the uncomfortable feeling that what must be done must be done and that what has been done cannot be undone. Banquo, who we come to feel is a threat to ourselves, however good, must be eliminated. So must Fleance, Macduff's wife and children, or anyone else who stands in the highway of our intense progress. Thinking that "to be thus is nothing, but to be safely thus," and wishing with "barefaced power" to sweep him from our sights, we straddle the play repelled by, but irresistibly drawn to Macbeth.

We listen to Macbeth as we listen to the beatings of our hearts. Engaged in the play, we think our hands are up to the wrists in blood and we startle at the knockings at our doors. Watching Macbeth, we suspect the height and depth of our own evil, testing ourselves up to the waist in the waters of some bloody lake. Allowed to do that which we must not do, guaranteed that we shall suffer for it, we watch Macbeth by laying our ears up against the door where our own silent nightmares are proceeding. There we see ourselves projected, gone somehow suddenly wrong, participating in the unforgivable, pursued by the unforgiving, which is most of all, ourselves.

Why should this be? Why are we so drawn to Macbeth by whom we must be at last repelled? Two reasons suggest themselves. First, we identify with Macbeth because identification is the condition of the theatre, especially in a nearly expressionistic play like *Macbeth* where the stage is the meeting ground between the hero's psyche and ours. Second, we pity Macbeth because, like us, he moves within breathing distance of innocence.

As moral obscurity is the world in which Macbeth stands at the beginning of his play, so it is the world in which we are seated watching the play, for the stage is both an extension of Macbeth's mind and the field of our imaginations. There in the domed, dimly lit theatre we watch like swaddled infants, this two hour's traffic, this our own strutting and fretting upon a bloody stage. Before us the Macbeths move like shadowy players, brief candles, little vaporous forms sliding behind a scrim. As if standing in Plato's cave, we see, but at one remove, we listen, but only to echoes, until we find ourselves fumbling along the corridors of our own dark psyches. There, supping on evil, dipped to the waist in blood, we watch the Macbeths go out at last in a clatter of sound, pursued by furies. The play over and the brief candles out, night flees, vapors vanish, and light is restored.

We identify with Macbeth because the theatre makes us suffer the illusion that we are Macbeth. We pity him because, like us, he stands next to innocence in a world in which evil is a prerequisite for being human. Macbeth is not motivelessly malicious like Richard III or Iago. He savors no sadistic pleasure in cruelty. Rather, set within reach of glory, he reaches and falls, and falling he is sick with remorse.

To have a clear conscience is to stand in the sun. To have a clouded conscience, one hovering between good and evil, between desire and restraint, is to stand where most of us stand, in that strange and obscure purgatory where the wind is pocketed with hot and cool trends, where the air is not nimble and sweet but fair and foul. This is the world of choice where thought and act and hand and eye are knit, but in a system of checks and balances.

Set within reach of triumph, who is not tempted to reach? And who, plucking one, will not compulsively and helplessly pluck every apple from the apple tree? For the line dividing self-preservation from ambition is often thin and we walk as if on a narrow cord above an abyss. We have constantly to choose, almost against our wills, for good, for as it is easier to fall than fly, so it is easier to be like Satan than God. We identify with Macbeth because we live in a dangerous world where a slip is likely to be a fall; but in the end, we must rip ourselves from him violently, as of a curse, as of an intolerable knowledge of ourselves. Through him we pay our chief debts to the unthinkable and are washed, when we wake, up onto the white shores of our own innocence. Macbeth is an ironic Christ who absorbs our sins that we may return "striding the blast." Redeemed through him, we ourselves must become the redeemers.

—Lisa Low, "Ridding Ourselves of Macbeth," *Massachusetts Review* 24, No. 4 (Winter 1983): 826–28

JOHN TURNER ON MACBETH'S HUBRIS

[John Turner (b. 1944) is the author of two books cowritten with Graham Holderness and Nick Potter, *Shakespeare: The Play of History* (1987) and *Shakespeare out of Court: Dramatizations of Court Society* (1990). In this extract, from the first of these books, Turner discusses Macbeth's hubris (a Greek concept meaning "excessive pride"), showing how this quality brings down both Macbeth and his kingdom.]

⟨. . .⟩ it is perhaps the psychological exploration of mistrust that is most remarkable in the play, as we watch Macbeth himself disintegrate within the disintegration of his kingdom and his family. 'For mine own good', he says, 'All causes shall give way' (III.iv.134–5). His hubris is a vain attempt to code the moral universe in his own desires in order to secure himself against his fears; and as the play goes on, he falls increasingly into the mistrustful anxieties of the paranoid cycle, where the magical sense of omnipotence is haunted by its fellow-contrary nightmare of impotence. As in *King Lear*, the single state of man falls into extremes which (to quote King James once more) 'although they seeme contrarie, yet growing to the height, runne euer both in one'. The copresence of these two extremes is embodied with great dramatic economy in the *double entendre* of the sisters' second group of prophecies, which torture Macbeth with the hope that that which it is impossible to prevent (his defeat) will be indeed prevented by that which is—again—impossible (the movement of Birnam Wood to Dunsinane, the existence of a man not born of woman). For Macbeth, these gnomic gobbets torn from the book of the black arts serve as fetishes; tantalizingly untrustworthy as they are, they encourage him to plunge on through his 'initiate fear' (III.iv.142) into a reckless debauchery of wrongdoing. But, in the manner of fetishes, they cannot adequately replace those reciprocities of love and trust which Macbeth has already put to the sword; they can do no more than afford a displaced ground upon which the subsequent conflict between desire and terror can be acted out to its inescapable conclusion. Finally, the contamination of this violent conflict infects Macbeth totally; the diminishing returns of his perversity wither him into the image of the 'wither'd Murther' that he had at first invoked; and then, played out, he is killed, a haunting after-image of the soldier in Act I, fighting fiercely still but for what he no longer believes in.

The process of Macbeth's disintegration is complemented by the integration of the thanes' resistance to him. They resist as they must; but we should not think simply of the opposition between them. There is identity as well as difference, and the language of the thanes suggests how deeply they are united with Macbeth in the strife which divides them; for the violence of emotion aroused by the murder of Duncan has caused a general moral panic throughout the community.

> Alas, poor country!
> Almost afraid to know itself. It cannot
> Be call'd our mother, but our grave; where nothing,
> But who knows nothing, is once seen to smile;
> Where sighs, and groans, and shrieks that rent the air
> Are made, not mark'd; where violent sorrow seems
> A modern ecstasy. . . .   (IV.iii.164–70)

Here is the same contamination of excitement and theatricality of imagination that we found in Macbeth, as Rosse attempts to picture the masterpiece of confusion that he sees in Scotland.

Yet, as Macduff found an old language to save himself from strangeness when he spoke of 'most sacrilegious Murther', so too do the thanes in their attempt to help their poor country reknow itself. It is an excited, often superstitious language, anathematizing Evil and the inversion of Good and sentimental-izing both because of the excitements that they feel. Their army will 'dew the sovereign flower, and drown the weeds' (V.ii.30), Macbeth is simply 'the tyrant' (l.11) and Malcolm 'the med'cine of the sickly weal' (l. 27): Macbeth is the source of all contamination in the realm, it seems, and to kill him has become a sacred necessity; and a regular use of images of purification and purgation accordingly marks the sacrificial way in which the thanes approach their military mission.

> Well; march we on,
> To give obedience where 'tis truly ow'd:
> Meet we the med'cine of the sickly weal;
> And with him pour we, in our country's purge,
> Each drop of us.   (V.ii.25–9)

Yet the emotions in Macduff, for one, are clearly not always of this sacrificial cast. 'Revenges burn in them' (l. 3), says Menteith of Malcolm and his military commanders, including 'the good Macduff' (l. 2). The language of purification is no doubt psychologically and politically valuable to restrain the violent energies of the civil war in which the play (as it began) is ending; and yet it is a language inadequate to what we see. There is a real sense in which Macbeth has become, despite all his tyranny, a scapegoat, bearing all the violence in his society, unifying it by his death and thereby preventing the thanes from understanding those political contradictions and psychological ambivalences that have caused the violence in which they are even now implicated. Duncan perceived the kind of violence by which he was threatened but could not accommodate it in either his language or his statecraft; Macbeth perceived the kind of violence by which he was threatened but could not accommodate its power to excite; but the thanes do no more than name the violence by which they are threatened 'Macbeth' and try to restore the world as it was before.

This desire on the part of the thanes to restore the world that had already failed them serves by contrast to reinforce the aristocratic heroism of Macbeth, a heroism not of service but of hubris.

> I am in blood
> Stepp'd in so far, that, should I wade no more,
> Returning were as tedious as go o'er. (III.iv.135–7)

Macbeth does not return, he goes over; he dares those perverse extremes of experience which he cannot resist. With a warrior's recklessness and a thane's conscience, he commits himself to the conflicts that they entail, and in so doing he draws out everything previously disavowed in his society. In daring that which was most forbidden, he sets in train a violent civil conflict that will change it decisively; he becomes the heroic destroyer of a heroic age.

—John Turner, "The Tyrannical Kingship of Macbeth," *Shakespeare: The Play of History* by Graham Holderness, Nick Potter and John Turner (Iowa City: University of Iowa Press, 1987), pp. 141–43

BARBARA EVERETT ON THE MACBETHS AS A MARRIED COUPLE

[Barbara Everett is a Senior Research Fellow and Lecturer in English at Somerville College, Oxford. She is the author of *Auden* (1964), *Poets in Their Time: Essays on English Poetry from Donne to Larkin* (1986), and editions of *Antony and Cleopatra* (1964) and *All's Well That Ends Well* (1970). In this extract, from her collection of essays on Shakespeare, *Young Hamlet* (1989), Everett studies the Macbeths' devotion to each other in their marriage, showing how this very devotion helps to bring about their downfall.]

In a recent interview about his production of *Macbeth*, Sir Peter Hall remarked—and he said it several times, with insistence—that Lady Macbeth is 'very, very sexy'. I find this modish jazzing up of the part saddening; it almost ideally misses by overshooting the real point of the darkly ironical fact that the Macbeths are probably Shakespeare's most thoroughly married couple. Not just lecherous but married: and these aren't the same things. The Macbeths have an extraordinary community and complicity. Some of the play's most troubling moments are those which reach ahead through (say) Chekhov and Ibsen and Strindberg, and many current writers, into 'the woe that is in marriage': the Macbeths become that terrible couple who appear so early in the play, 'two spent Swimmers, that doe cling together, / And choake their Art'—their love is so corrupted by the struggle to survive as to pull each other down. Macbeth, to put it simply, loves Lady Macbeth;—they love each other; at the painful III.ii, where they first show a marked drift away from each other, each minds. Macbeth addresses his wife with troubled extra care, as 'Love', 'deare Wife', and 'dearest Chuck'. The tragic mutual destructiveness of the marriage is summed up by a simple fact. Married couples invariably, if it is a true marriage, grow like each other. The Macbeths slowly exchange qualities in the course of the play. From the beginning Lady Macbeth has brought to their life a directness, a practicality, an inability to see difficulties in a good cause. Only, she can't see difficulties in a bad cause, either. 'But screw your courage to the sticking place, / And wee'le not fayle.' The crux over what precisely her first 'We faile?' means is interesting: she genuinely can't imagine—she can't cope with ifs; she simply throws Macbeth's phrases back at him. And this practicality moves into Macbeth in the form of brutality—which is why he starts not to need her any more. Lady Macbeth for her part inherits his imagination, but only in the form of nightmare. And she can't live with it: it stops her sleeping ever again.

I want to stress the fact of Shakespeare's depth and seriousness and even tenderness in depicting their marriage. One of the play's most touching and subtle moments is that which brings Lady Macbeth before us for the first time, and she is reading Macbeth's letter: he exists for her when he isn't there. He exists too much for her when he isn't there, she plans and thinks ahead too much for him, she too much connives, putting her image of Macbeth's future where her conscience should be: as the Doctor says, staring at her wide-open but out-of-touch gaze, 'You have knowne what you should not.' And the Gentlewoman adds, 'Heaven knowes what she has knowne.' Lady Macbeth is Macbeth's 'Dearest Partner of Greatnesse', the tender yet arrogant phrase Macbeth uses to her in his letter, as if the one thing in the world a good marriage were for, were getting a throne. And there begins from that point the insidious corruption of the good which I mentioned earlier:

> yet I doe feare thy Nature,
> It is too full o'th' Milke of humane kindnesse,
> To catch the neerest way . . .

For Lady Macbeth's immediate action, when she knows that the King is coming, is to call to spirits to 'Unsex me here'—to make herself no more a woman. She is sacrificing to Macbeth's success his succession—their hope of children. When the two of them meet at I. vii, it is the hope of children, and the destruction of children, that is a theme of what they say to each other. There is a kind of strange sense in the fact that when finally—in V. v—Lady Macbeth dies, evidently by her own hand, Macbeth feels her death as real, yet as 'signifying nothing'. He has created a present in which there is no time for death. Because he has succeeded, he cannot grieve for the one person he cared for absolutely, the person who was in a strict and technical sense 'his life'.

> —Barbara Everett, "Macbeth: Succeeding," *Young Hamlet: Essays on Shakespeare's Tragedies* (Oxford: Clarendon Press, 1989), pp. 103–5

CHARLES AND MICHELLE MARTINDALE ON DEATH IN *MACBETH*

[Charles Martindale (b. 1949) is a professor of classics at the University of Bristol in England. He has written *Milton and the Transformation of Ancient Epic* (1986) and *Redeeming the Text: Latin Poetry and the Hermeneutics of Reception* (1993). With his wife, Michelle Martindale (b. 1951), he has written *Shakespeare and the Uses of Antiquity* (1990), from which the following extract is taken. The Martindales discuss the reactions of various characters in *Macbeth* to death, maintaining that these reactions reflect the attitude to death exemplified by the Stoic philosophers of classical antiquity.]

In *Macbeth* reactions to disaster involving both contempt of death and a readiness to accept whatever happens can be seen to some extent in the light of Stoic philosophy. According to Seneca, in his 26th letter to Lucilius, on old age and death, *egregia res est mortem condiscere* ('it is an excellent thing to learn how to die'). Language like this lies at the root of the description of the execution of the Thane of Cawdor, who dies 'as one that had been studied in his death, / To throw away the dearest thing he owed / As 'twere a careless trifle' (I.iv. 9–11). Though Cawdor is a traitor, his courage is seen as admirable, and this helps to set the tone of this tough work, in which such courageous self-control is almost the only virtue one might dare to trust in or hope for. It to an extent redeems Cawdor's treachery, and in the end restores a certain stature to Macbeth, when he abandons the last vestiges of pretence and goes down fighting. Between these points are shown a series of responses to the news of a death which closely concerns the hearer. All of them, except the last, are in some way unbalanced, lacking the poise that can express true feeling for the deceased.

Macduff reacts to the discovery of Duncan's body in terms of Last Judgement imagery, mixed with horrified gasps (II.iii.62ff.). There is no personal sorrow here. One of the effects of Macbeth's actions is that a balanced individuality of grief is hardly achievable. Everything is swallowed up in enormity. Malcolm and Donalbain are quite unable to make any proper response to their father's death. Malcolm's immediate question 'O, by whom?' (98) is notorious for its inadequacy, but little else is possible. The answers multiply falsehood and specula-tion. When the brothers next speak, it is stealthily to each other. Their fear for their own lives preoccupies them; they feel in no mind to express any sorrow publicly, and even to themselves they can say nothing of emotional substance (117ff.).

Much deserved admiration has been accorded to the way Shakespeare portrays Macduff when he receives the news of the slaughter of his family (IV.iii.199ff.). The episode is characterized by a powerful depiction of grief, from Macduff's initial inability to absorb the news to his brushing aside of Malcolm's heroic exhortation to 'make us medicines of our great revenge'. For all the human intelligibility of Macduff's behaviour, however, it is not put forward as a model for conduct, even in these circumstances. His response to the disaster is complicated by his feelings of guilt about his contribution to it, and, lacking a wholesome conscience, he is tossed between extremes of fury and despair. If, as we are inclined to believe, because of the way it fits into the immediate context, Macduff's exclamation 'He has no children' (216) does refer to Macbeth, and to the impossibility of effecting a proper vengeance because he has no children for Macduff to kill, then it is a glimpse of a hell as deep, though brief, as any of Macbeth's own. The enormity of what Macbeth has done proves infectious in so many ways. And Macbeth himself, of course, can find no other way to react to the news of his wife's death than an impatient shrug, followed by an over-eloquent generalization on the human condition, which tells us a great deal about himself, but expresses nothing at all of loss or mourning (V.v.17ff.). There is no sense of any communication, sharing of suffering, just of dissatisfaction in isolation. He does not even ask what happened.

The only balanced response in the play to news of death comes near the end, in an episode which is often underestimated, both as regards its structural importance and its intrinsic power to move. Old Siward's immediate response to hearing of the death of his son in battle is to ask how he died. On learning that Young Siward received his wounds 'on the front', and therefore died fighting bravely, he says:

> Why then, God's soldier be he!
> Had I as many sons as I have hairs,
> I would not wish them to a fairer death!
> And so, his knell is knolled.   (V.ix.13–16)

Old Siward should not be thought of as heartless. The grief which he refuses to pour out in public is clearly hinted at by Malcolm: 'He's worth more sorrow, / And that I'll spend for him'. But Old Siward can cap this: 'He's worth no more; / They say he parted well and paid his score: / And so, God be with him!' The sense of rightness and fruition expressed here should not be easily brushed aside. At last the time is free, and heroic response to loss is once more possible. Like the Thane of Cawdor, Young Siward died well, but also had the advantage of pursuing the good cause to the end. When the country is purged of Macbeth's wickedness, men can respond to death with a decent restraint and balance. Old Siward's reaction is that of a toughened, inured soldier, but then it is to a great extent on his type of standards that the play's moral foundations are laid.

—Charles and Michelle Martindale, *Shakespeare and the Uses of Antiquity: An Introductory Essay* (New York: Routledge, 1990), pp. 177–79

❖

NICHOLAS GRENE ON THE WITCHES IN *MACBETH*

[Nicholas Grene (b. 1947) is the author of *Synge: A Critical Study of the Plays* (1976), *Shakespeare, Jonson, Molière: The Comic Contract* (1980), and other volumes. In this extract, from his book, *Shakespeare's Tragic Imagination* (1992), Grene shows how the scene with the witches that opens *Macbeth* indicates that the supernatural is the terrain upon which the entire action of the play must function.]

The storm of thunder and lightning which attends the three Witches on their entrance into the first scene of *Macbeth* is not a natural phenomenon. When Lear asks his 'philosopher' Edgar 'what is the cause of thunder', it is an open question. The storm in *King Lear* is at once literal and metaphorical, wet rain that wets, thunder that will not 'peace' at the King's bidding, as well as the manifestation of those 'heavens' to which the characters look up so often and struggle to understand. In *Macbeth* there is no such duality. The Witches belong with the thunder and lightning, and the thunder and lightning with them, in unbreakable association as the theatrical signs of a non-natural supernature. The tiny twelve-line first scene of the play establishes the supernatural as a ground of reality prior to the human action. In *King Lear* the characters reach out from within a natural world to identify transcendent principles of good and evil to shape their experience—'is there any cause in nature that make these hard hearts?' In *Macbeth*, evil is manifestly there theatrically, other than, external to, the human beings to which it will appear in such equivocal and equivocating form. Which is not to say that such an extrinsic supernatural is absolutely to govern the drama that follows. It is rather that the mini-overture of the Witches signals the supernatural as one of the determining givens of the tragedy.

The Witches are certainly there and certainly evil at the start of *Macbeth*. In that knowledge we are given a position of privilege unlike the opening of *Hamlet* where, with the watchers on the battlements, we must await the appearance of the Ghost, and bewilderedly conjecture what the walking 'thing' in armour may be. Yet just *what* the ominous figures are omens of, *how* they are to relate to the actions we see initially, is made no clearer in *Macbeth* than in *Hamlet*. In the Witches' opening incantation there is a confused sense of conflict, 'hurly-burly' and 'battle', swirling around the single distinguishable name of Macbeth. Sure enough, I.ii begins with a 'bleeding captain' reporting from the battlefield, a figure of violence apparently to be linked to the Witches' apparition, just as the Ghost in *Hamlet* is associated by the watchers with the military preparations for coming war with Norway. But the Captain/Sergeant's reports turn out to be of victory on all fronts in which Macbeth is the illustrious hero. The Witches do not prefigure war, any more than the Ghost did. Our attention instead is projected, beyond the account of how 'the battle's lost and won', towards the meeting with Macbeth which will come after; as in *Hamlet*, the prefigured evil is diverted from the outer conflicts of war to the more inward violences of apparent peace.

—Nicholas Grene, *Shakespeare's Tragic Imagination* (New York: St. Martin's Press, 1992), pp. 193–94

GARRY WILLS ON *MACBETH* AND THE GUNPOWDER PLOT

[Garry Wills (b. 1934) is an adjunct professor of history at Northwestern University and one of the most prolific and respected political commentators of our time. Among his many books on American politics are *Nixon Agonistes* (1970), *Inventing America: Jefferson's Declaration of Independence* (1978), *The Kennedy Imprisonment: A Meditation on Power* (1982), *Reagan's America: The Innocents at Home* (1987), and *Under God: Religion in American Politics* (1990). But Wills has often turned his attention to literature; his first book (1961) was a study of G. K. Chesterton. In this extract, from his recent book on *Macbeth*, Wills studies the play in the context of the Gunpowder Plot of 1605, in which Catholic rebels attempted to blow up the Houses of Parliament.]

The death of the King is an apocalyptic event in *Macbeth*. Omens foretell "dire combustion and confus'd events' (2.3.58), and Macbeth says, of the crime's revelation (2.3.66–69):

> Confusion now hath made his masterpiece!
> Most sacrilegious Murther hath broke ope
> The Lord's anointed temple and stole thence
> The life of the building.

Confusion is the principle of the devil's reign, as order is of God's. Attendants on the Whore of Babylon tell her, in ⟨Thomas⟩ Dekker's play:

> On your brow, they say, is writ a name
> In letters mystical, which they interpret
> "Confusion." By Great Babylon they mean
> The City of Confusion.

Confusion occurs frequently in the Powder writings—from ⟨Sir Edward⟩ Coke's speeches to *The Devil of the Vault:*

> Confusion with hell's horrid howls
> Denounces grim death's alarms.

There is another use of "confusion" in *Macbeth*—at 3.5.29, where it means Macbeth's "damnation." This occurs in Hecate's speech, often deleted from modern performances ⟨. . .⟩

While Macduff has invoked Confusion, Macbeth—all of whose words over the deed *he* did are equivocal—says (2.3.95–96):

> The wine of life is drawn, and the mere lees
> Is left this vault to brag of.

Vault was the "grassy knoll" of Gunpowder writings. Macbeth draws an analogy; as heaven to earth, so Duncan's crime, in an upper world, to the lees in this underworld. Fawkes meant for the blood of the nation to be blown out of the upper hall of Parliament, leaving only the lesser breeds in the vault to inherit England.

One last aspect of Duncan's murder will be raised here, though it depends less on specific terms than on a whole cluster of words having to do with the penetration of secrets. James was praised over and over for his reading of the Plot's clues. But Shakespeare makes Duncan go to his death unsuspecting, with no alertness to the evil omens others become aware of. Duncan's *undiscerning* nature is emphasized by his own words (I.4.11–14):

> There's no art
> To find the mind's construction in the face.
> He was a gentleman on whom I built
> An absolute trust.

Nothing could be more at odds with the way James faced plots against him (not only the Powder Plot, but the Gowrie Plot, also commemorated in annual sermons that claimed he kept his head and baffled his assailants shrewdly). James *did* have an art to find the construction (construing) of deceptive appearances. He was a Joseph seeing through his brothers' lies, according to ⟨Lancelot⟩ Andrewes. He was like an angel looking through appearances, according to Coke. He was like a wiser Priam uncovering the trick of the Trojan Horse, according to Francis Herring: "The shrewd king, sifting each point in his quiet mind said at the end of his reflection: These clues are not to be treated lightly. . . .' "

The proof that audiences would pick up references to a king's shrewd dealing with the Plot is in Dekker's play, where the attempt to shoot Elizabeth as she strolls in her garden is preternaturally anticipated by the Queen (*The Whore of Babylon* 4.1.69–71):

> It came unto me strangely. From a window
> Mine eyes took mark of him; that he would shoot
> 'Twas told me, and I tried if he durst do it.

This is exactly the kind of inspired hunch that came to James— but not to Duncan. Critics have often expressed surprise that Shakespeare's troupe would put on at James's court the story of a Scottish king's assassination. But Shakespeare went out of his way to show how different Duncan was from the picture of James being spread energetically through all the media just when *Macbeth* was first played. It is not enough to read *Macbeth* in isolation. We have to know something about what else was being said, sung, and staged at the time. We have to be sensitive to language that bristled with the ideology of the period. So far we have just dipped into some of the scattered terms in that language. The larger patterns connected with the Plot—with equivocation, Jesuitry, and witches—call for ampler exploration.

—Garry Wills, *Witches and Jesuits: Shakespeare's* Macbeth (New York: New York Public Library/Oxford University Press, 1995), pp. 29–31

Works by William Shakespeare

Venus and Adonis. 1593.

The Rape of Lucrece. 1594.

Henry VI. 1594.

Titus Andronicus. 1594.

The Taming of the Shrew. 1594.

Romeo and Juliet. 1597.

Richard III. 1597.

Richard II. 1597.

Love's Labour's Lost. 1598.

Henry IV. 1598.

The Passionate Pilgrim. 1599.

A Midsummer Night's Dream. 1600.

The Merchant of Venice. 1600.

Much Ado about Nothing. 1600.

Henry V. 1600.

The Phoenix and the Turtle. 1601.

The Merry Wives of Windsor. 1602.

Hamlet. 1603.

King Lear. 1608.

Troilus and Cressida. 1609.

Sonnets. 1609.

Pericles. 1609.

Othello. 1622.

Mr. William Shakespeares Comedies, Histories & Tragedies. Ed. John Heminge and Henry Condell. 1623 (First Folio), 1632 (Second Folio), 1663 (Third Folio), 1685 (Fourth Folio).

Poems. 1640.

Works. Ed. Nicholas Rowe. 1709. 6 vols.

Works. Ed. Alexander Pope. 1723–25. 6 vols.

Works. Ed. Lewis Theobald. 1733. 7 vols.

Works. Ed. Thomas Hanmer. 1743–44. 6 vols.

Works. Ed. William Warburton. 1747. 8 vols.

Plays. Ed. Samuel Johnson. 1765. 8 vols.

Plays and Poems. Ed. Edmond Malone. 1790. 10 vols.

The Family Shakespeare. Ed. Thomas Bowdler. 1807. 4 vols.

Works. Ed. J. Payne Collier. 1842–44. 8 vols.

Works. Ed. H. N. Hudson. 1851–56. 11 vols.

Works. Ed. Alexander Dyce. 1857. 6 vols.

Works. Ed. Richard Grant White. 1857–66. 12 vols.

Works (Cambridge Edition). Ed. William George Clark, John Glover, and William Aldis Wright. 1863–66. 9 vols.

A New Variorum Edition of the Works of Shakespeare. Ed. H. H. Furness et al. 1871– .

Works. Ed. W. J. Rolfe. 1871–96. 40 vols.

The Pitt Press Shakespeare. Ed. A. W. Verity. 1890–1905. 13 vols.

The Warwick Shakespeare. 1893–1938. 13 vols.

The Temple Shakespeare. Ed. Israel Gollancz. 1894–97. 40 vols.

The Arden Shakespeare. Ed. W. J. Craig, R. H. Case et al. 1899–1924. 37 vols.

The Shakespeare Apocrypha. Ed. C. F. Tucker Brooke. 1908.

The Yale Shakespeare. Ed. Wilbur L. Cross, Tucker Brooke, and Willard Highley Durham. 1917–27. 40 vols.

The New Shakespeare (Cambridge Edition). Ed. Arthur Quiller-Couch and John Dover Wilson. 1921–62. 38 vols.

The New Temple Shakespeare. Ed. M. R. Ridley. 1934–36. 39 vols.

Works. Ed. George Lyman Kittredge. 1936.

The Penguin Shakespeare. Ed. G. B. Harrison. 1937–59. 36 vols.

The New Clarendon Shakespeare. Ed. R. E. C. Houghton. 1938– .

The Arden Shakespeare. Ed. Una Ellis-Fermor et al. 1951– .

The Complete Pelican Shakespeare. Ed. Alfred Harbage. 1969.

The Complete Signet Classic Shakespeare. Ed. Sylvan Barnet. 1972.

The Oxford Shakespeare. Ed. Stanley Wells. 1982– .

The New Cambridge Shakespeare. Ed. Philip Brockbank. 1984– .

Works about William Shakespeare and *Macbeth*

Adelman, Janet. " 'Born of Woman': Fantasies of Maternal Power in *Macbeth*." In *Cannibals, Witches, and Divorce: Estranging the Renaissance,* ed. Marjorie Garber. Baltimore: Johns Hopkins University Press, 1987, pp. 90–121.

Asp, Carolyn. " 'Be Bloody, Bold and Resolute': Tragic Action and Sexual Stereotyping in *Macbeth*." *Studies in Philology* 78 (1981): 153–69.

Baird, David. *The Thane of Cawdor: A Detective Study of* Macbeth. London: Oxford University Press, 1937.

Barroll, J. Leeds. *Artificial Persons: The Formation of Character in the Tragedies of Shakespeare.* Columbia: University of South Carolina Press, 1974.

Bartholomeusz, Dennis. *Macbeth and the Players.* Cambridge: Cambridge University Press, 1969.

Berger, Harry, Jr. "The Early Scenes of *Macbeth:* Preface to a New Interpretation." *ELH* 47 (1980): 1–31.

Booth, Wayne C. "Macbeth as Tragic Hero." *Journal of General Education* 6 (1951–52): 17–25.

Brown, John Russell, ed. *Focus on* Macbeth. London: Routledge & Kegan Paul, 1982.

Bulman, James C. *The Heroic Idiom of Shakespearean Tragedy.* Newark: University of Delaware Press, 1985.

Calderwood, James L. *If It Were Done:* Macbeth *and Tragic Action.* Amherst: University of Massachusetts Press, 1986.

———. "*Macbeth:* Counter-*Hamlet*." *Shakespeare Studies* 17 (1985): 103–21.

Charlton, H. B. *Shakespearian Tragedy.* Cambridge: Cambridge University Press, 1948.

Clark, Arthur Melville. *Murder under Trust; or, The Tropical Macbeth and Other Jacobean Matters.* Edinburgh: Scottish Academic Press, 1981.

Cox, Roger L. "Macbeth Divided against Himself." In Cox's *Between Earth and Heaven: Shakespeare, Dostoevsky, and the Meaning of Christian Tragedy.* New York: Holt, Rinehart & Winston, 1969, pp. 96–119.

Dillon, Janette. *Shakespeare and the Solitary Man.* Totowa, NJ: Rowman & Littlefield, 1981, pp. 135–45.

Eagleton, Terry. *Shakespeare and Society: Critical Studies in Shakespearean Drama.* New York: Schocken Books, 1967.

Egan, Robert. "His Hour upon the Stage: Role-Playing in *Macbeth.*" *Centennial Review* 22 (1978): 143–67.

Elliott, G. R. *Dramatic Providence in* Macbeth. 2nd ed. Princeton: Princeton University Press, 1960.

Empson, William. "*Macbeth.*" In Empson's *Essays on Shakespeare.* Ed. David B. Pirie. Cambridge: Cambridge University Press, 1986, pp. 137–57.

Farnham, Willard. *Shakespeare's Tragic Frontier: The World of His Final Tragedies.* Berkeley: University of California Press, 1950.

Fergusson, Sir James. *The Man behind Macbeth and Other Studies.* London: Faber & Faber, 1969.

Foster, Donald W. "*Macbeth's* War on Time." *English Literary Renaissance* 16 (1986): 319–42.

Fox, Alice. "Obstetrics and Gynecology in *Macbeth.*" *Shakespeare Studies* 12 (1973): 127–41.

Ghose, Zulfikar. *Shakespeare's Mortal Knowledge: A Reading of the Tragedies.* Basingstoke, UK: Macmillan Press, 1993.

Goldman, Michael. *Acting and Action in Shakespearean Tragedy.* Princeton: Princeton University Press, 1985.

Greene, James J. "Macbeth: Masculinity as Murder." *American Imago* 41 (1984): 155–80.

Harrison, G. B. *Shakespeare's Tragedies.* London: Routledge & Kegan Paul, 1951.

Hawkes, Terence. *Shakespeare and the Reason.* London: Routledge & Kegan Paul, 1964.

Heilman, Robert B. "The Criminal as Tragic Hero." *Shakespeare Survey* 19 (1966): 12–24.

Hobson, Alan. *Full Circle: Shakespeare and Moral Development.* London: Chatto & Windus, 1972.

Holland, Norman N. *The Shakespearean Imagination.* New York: Macmillan, 1964.

Holloway, John. *The Story of the Night: Studies in Shakespeare's Major Tragedies.* London: Routledge & Kegan Paul, 1961.

Jekels, Ludwig. "The Riddle of Shakespeare's Macbeth." *Psychoanalytic Review* 30 (1943): 361–85.

Jones, Emrys. *Scenic Form in Shakespeare.* Oxford: Clarendon Press, 1971.

Jorgensen, Paul A. *Our Naked Frailties: Sensational Art and Meaning in* Macbeth. Berkeley: University of California Press, 1971.

Kilman, Bernice W. *Macbeth.* Manchester, UK: Manchester University Press, 1992.

Kimbrough, Robert. "Macbeth: The Prisoner of Gender." *Shakespeare Studies* 16 (1983): 175–90.

Kirsch, Arthur. "Macbeth's Suicide." *ELH* 51 (1984): 269–96.

Knight, G. Wilson. *Shakespeare's Dramatic Challenge: On the Rise of Shakespeare's Tragic Heroes.* London: Croom Helm; New York: Barnes & Noble, 1977.

Lawlor, John. *The Tragic Sense in Shakespeare.* London: Chatto & Windus, 1960.

Long, Michael. *Macbeth.* Boston: Twayne, 1989.

McAlindon, T. *Shakespeare and Decorum.* London: Macmillan, 1973.

————. *Shakespeare's Tragic Cosmos.* Cambridge: Cambridge University Press, 1991.

McElroy, Bernard. *Shakespeare's Mature Tragedies.* Princeton: Princeton University Press, 1973.

Mangan, Michael. *A Preface to Shakespeare's Tragedies.* London: Longman, 1991.

Margolies, David. *Monsters of the Deep: Social Dissolution in Shakespeare's Tragedies.* Manchester: Manchester University Press, 1992.

Moorthy, P. Rama. "Fear in *Macbeth.*" *Essays in Criticism* 23 (1973): 154–66.

Morris, Ivor. *Shakespeare's God: The Role of Religion in the Tragedies.* London: George Allen & Unwin, 1972.

Nevo, Ruth. *Tragic Form in Shakespeare.* Princeton: Princeton University Press, 1972.

Norbrook, David. "*Macbeth* and the Politics of Historiography." In *Politics of Discourse: The Literature and History of Seventeenth-Century England,* ed. Kevin Sharpe and Stephen N. Zwicker. Berkeley: University of California Press, 1987, pp. 78–116.

Parker, Barbara L. "*Macbeth:* The Great Illusion." *Sewanee Review* 78 (1970): 476–87.

Paul, Anthony. *The Torture of the Mind:* Macbeth, *Tragedy and Chiasmus.* Amsterdam: Thesis Publishers, 1992.

Paul, Henry N. *The Royal Play of* Macbeth. New York: Macmillan, 1950.

Prosner, Matthew N. *The Heroic Image in Five Shakespearean Tragedies.* Princeton: Princeton University Press, 1965.

Ramsey, Jarold. "The Perversion of Manliness in *Macbeth.*" *Studies in English Literature* 1500–1900 13 (1973): 285–300.

Ribner, Irving. *Patterns in Shakespearian Tragedy.* London: Methuen, 1960.

Rogers, H. L. *"Double Profit" in* Macbeth. Melbourne: Melbourne University Press, 1964.

Rosenberg, Marvin. *The Masks of Macbeth.* Berkeley: University of California Press, 1978.

Ryan, Kiernan. *Shakespeare.* Atlantic Highlands, NJ: Humanities Press, 1989.

Sanders, Wilbur. *The Dramatist and the Received Idea: Studies in the Plays of Marlowe and Shakespeare.* Cambridge: Cambridge University Press, 1968.

Schoenbaum, S., ed. Macbeth: *Critical Essays.* New York: Garland, 1991.

Sewell, Arthur. *Character and Society in Shakespeare.* Oxford: Clarendon Press, 1951.

Shakespeare Survey 19 (1966). Special *Macbeth* issue.

Sinfield, Alan. "*Macbeth:* History, Ideology and Intellectuals." *Critical Quarterly* 28 (1986): 63–77.

Smidt, Kristian. *Unconformities in Shakespeare's Tragedies.* New York: St. Martin's Press, 1990.

Smith, Molly. *The Darker World Within: Evil in the Tragedies of Shakespeare and His Successors.* Newark: University of Delaware Press, 1991.

Stachniewski, John. "Calvinist Psychology in *Macbeth.*" *Shakespeare Studies* 20 (1988): 169–89.

Stockholder, Kay. *Dream Works: Lovers and Families in Shakespeare's Plays.* Toronto: University of Toronto Press, 1987.

Sypher, Wylie. *The Ethic of Time: Structures of Experience in Shakespeare.* New York: Seabury Press, 1976.

Turner, John. *Macbeth.* Buckingham, UK: Open University Press, 1992.

Walker, Roy. *The Time Is Free: A Study of* Macbeth. London: Andrew Dakers, 1949.

Watkins, Ronald, and Jeremy Lemmon. *Macbeth.* Newton Abbot, UK: David & Charles, 1974.

Wilburn, David. "Phantasmagoric *Macbeth.*" *English Literary Renaissance* 16 (1986): 520–49.

Wilson, Harold S. *On the Design of Shakespearean Tragedy.* Toronto: University of Toronto Press, 1957.

Index of
Themes and Ideas

AMBITION and its role in the play, 7, 14–15, 18, 22, 23, 24, 27, 28, 29, 32, 34, 38, 40, 48–49, 55

ARIEL (*The Tempest*) compared to the Weird Sisters, 33

BANQUO: as a ghost, 19, 26, 37, 45; and his role in the play, 14, 16, 17–18, 20, 23, 25–26, 29, 35, 38–39, 41–42, 44, 54

BIRNAM WOOD and its role in the play, 20, 21, 22, 35, 42, 44, 57

CALIBAN (*The Tempest*) compared to the Weird Sisters, 33

CAPTAIN/SERGEANT, THE, and his role in the play, 13, 14, 51, 65

CAWDOR, THANE OF, and his role in the play, 13, 44, 62, 64

CLAUDIUS (*Hamlet*) compared to Macbeth, 5, 7

CHRONICLES (Holinshed) as a source for the play, 43–45, 51

DAGGER, Macbeth's vision of, 16, 19, 49

DOCTOR, THE, and his role in the play, 21, 61

DONALBAIN, PRINCE OF SCOTLAND, and his role in the play, 13, 17, 62

DUNCAN, KING OF SCOTLAND: as father figure to Macbeth, 6, 13, 34, 38–39; and his role in the play, 14–17, 18, 21, 23, 25, 29, 30, 37, 41, 51, 53, 57–59, 61, 62, 66–68

EDMUND (*King Lear*) compared to Macbeth, 5

EDWARD, KING OF ENGLAND, and his role in the play, 19, 20–21, 25

ELIZABETH I, QUEEN OF ENGLAND, and her relation to Shakespeare and his plays, 9, 10, 38, 68

EVIL as a theme, 34, 40–41, 45–46, 49, 50, 53, 54, 55, 58, 65, 67

FLEANCE and his role in the play, 5, 16, 17, 18, 20, 26, 39, 54

GONERIL (*King Lear*) compared to Lady Macbeth, 46, 53

HAMLET (*Hamlet*) compared to Macbeth, 5, 7, 36, 54

HAMLET and how it compares, 31–32, 65–66

HECATE and her role in the play, 7, 24, 67

IAGO (*Othello*) compared to Macbeth, 5, 36, 55

IMAGINATION as a theme, 5–7, 40, 50, 60

JAMES I, KING OF ENGLAND, and his relation to Shakespeare and his plays, 10, 38, 44, 57, 67–68

KING LEAR and how it compares, 54–55, 64–65

LEAR (*King Lear*) compared to Macbeth, 5, 36, 54

LENNOX and his role in the play, 17, 20

MACBETH: audience's identification with, 5–6, 27, 29–31, 49–50, 54–56; as a "butcher," 51–53; and his role in the play, 13–24, 27–28, 32, 38–43, 45–48, 60–65; as a tyrant, 34–35, 57–59

MACBETH, LADY: infertility of, 34, 38–39, 61; insanity and suicide of, 21, 30, 36–37; and her role in the play, 7, 15–19, 24, 27, 29, 32, 34, 41, 48–50, 53, 59–60, 63

MACBETH: in its historical context, 15, 21, 38, 43–45, 66–68; structure of, 13–23, 27, 31, 40, 47, 65–66; as a tragedy, 5, 32; uses of language in, 32, 35–37, 46

MACDONWALD and his role in the play, 13, 23, 44, 53

MACDUFF, THANE OF FIFE, and his role in the play, 17, 19–23, 25, 35, 39, 45, 51, 58, 62–63, 67

MACDUFF'S FAMILY, the murder of, 5, 20, 21, 25, 37, 39, 54, 63

MALCOLM, PRINCE OF SCOTLAND, and his role in the play, 13, 15, 17, 19, 20, 22, 23, 25, 45, 46, 51, 58, 62–64

MIDSUMMER NIGHT'S DREAM, A, and how it compares, 5

MOBY-DICK (Melville) and how it compares, 6–7

MORTALITY as a theme, 19, 38, 62–64

OPHELIA (*Hamlet*) compared to Lady Macbeth, 36, 37

OTHELLO (*Othello*) compared to Macbeth, 5, 36

OTHELLO and how it compares, 50

PORTER, THE, and his role in the play, 17, 31, 36

RAPE OF LUCRECE and how it compares, 47

RICHARD III (*Richard III*) compared to Macbeth, 7, 28–31, 55

ROMEO (*Romeo and Juliet*) compared to Macbeth, 54

ROSSE, THANE OF, and his role in the play, 13, 17, 20, 51, 58

SHAKESPEARE, WILLIAM: acceptance of traditional gender roles by, 51, 53; dramatic technique of, 14, 36, 49–50, 63, 67–68; life of, 8–11; punning of, 32

SIWARDS, THE, and their role in the play, 22, 63–64

STORM, symbolism of, 13, 14, 23, 64–65

SUCCESSION as a theme, 7, 18, 26, 29, 38–39, 42, 52, 61

SUPERNATURAL, THE, as a theme, 5–7, 16, 28, 29, 30, 32, 40, 49, 58, 64–68

TEMPEST, THE, and how it compares, 5

THANES, THE, and their role in the play, 7, 35, 57–59

WEIRD SISTERS, THE: and their role in the play, 7, 17, 18, 19, 21, 24–25, 28, 33, 34, 38–39, 41, 42, 44, 57, 64–66, 68; as forces of disorder, 13, 14, 23